HOW THE CATHOLIC CHURCH
IS GOVERNED

HOW THE CATHOLIC CHURCH IS GOVERNED

HEINRICH SCHARP

HERDER AND HERDER

This translation by Annelise Derrick is based on the original German version

of "Wie die Kirche regiert wird" published by Josef Knecht,

Carolusdruckerei GmbH. ,Frankfurt am Main ,4th edition 1954

Second impression published 1960 by

Herder and Herder, Inc.

7 West 46th Street, New York 36, N. Y.

Library of Congress Catalog Card Number: 60-6658

© 1960 by Herder KG

Made and printed by Herder Druck, Freiburg, West Gemany

11121558

CONTENTS

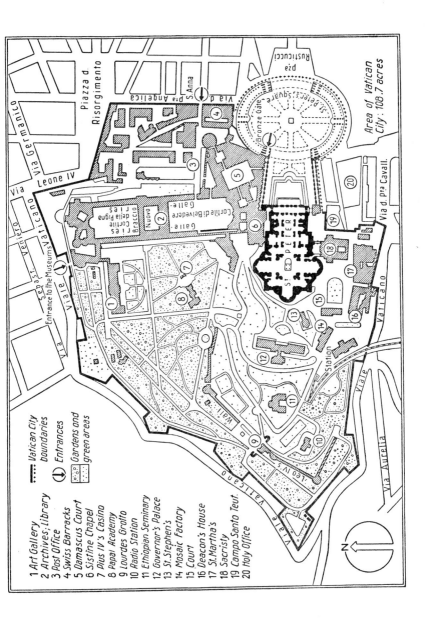

1 Art Gallery
2 Archives, Library
3 Post Office
4 Swiss Barracks
5 Damascus Court
6 Sistine Chapel
7 Pius IV's Casino
8 Papal Academy
9 Lourdes Grotto
10 Radio Station
11 Ethiopian Seminary
12 Governor's Palace
13 St. Stephen's
14 Mosaic Factory
15 Court
16 Deacon's House
17 St. Martha's
18 Sacristy
19 Campo Santo Teut.
20 Holy Office

····· Vatican City boundaries
Ⓛ Entrances
Gardens and green areas

Area of Vatican City: 108.7 acres

St. Peter's Square
Bronze Gate
Pza Rusticucci

Via d. Pta Angelica
S. Anna
Piazza d. Risorgimento

Via Germanico
Via Leone IV
Via Sepstr. Veniero
Via Vaticano
Entrance to the Museums
Viale

Cortile della Pigna
Galle. Nuovo
Cortile di Belvedere
Galle. Lres Braccia
Galle.

Wall
Station
Viale Leone IV
Viale Vaticano
Via Aurelia
Via d. Pta Cavall.

N

No one will ever forget the experience of being present in St. Peter's when the Pope enters for the solemn High Mass of Easter Day. All the magnificence, all the glory of the Church, the light, the colour, the music and rejoicing join in one incomparable harmony. As the trumpets of the Noble Guard ring out from the gallery above the great west doors all the lights go on – innumerable delicate *lustri* of cut glass shining from the pillars and the arches, from the great curve of the dome and the deep recesses of the apse. The red damask hangings with their narrow gold borders, extending from the cornices to the floor, seem to be soaked in the warm glow of colour. The dome rises darkly above the brilliance of the light as though unsupported. Bernini's bronze baldacchino, towering in the strong rhythm of the Baroque above the papal altar, seems to echo like a powerful chord through the basilica. Ninety-three lamps are always burning by the marble balustrade of the *confessio,* above St. Peter's tomb; over to the right, on this great day, the time-darkened bronze statue of St. Peter stiffly and solemnly wears a red cope, embroidered in gold, and the triple crown of the tiara. The Pope's Palatine Guard – good-natured citizens of Rome, butchers and bakers, shoe-makers and shop-keepers who have donned a brightly-coloured uniform with a peaked military cap for today's honourable duty and whose work it is to keep the central aisle free from the lively congregation – proudly present arms with bayonets fixed. Nearer the doors stand the papal gendarmes – big broad-shouldered men in top-boots and white cavalry breeches, with heavy swords and splendid bearskins.

The solemn entry begins. First come Swiss Guards in their glistening steel breast-plates, with their plumed helmets and long halberds. The eye hardly has time to distinguish those who follow: the Apostolic Preacher and the Confessor of the Pontifical Court, the Procurators-General of the mendicant orders in the brown, black and white habits of those orders, the consistorial advocates, the Privy Chamberlains and Prelates, the Privy Chaplains carring the Pope's mitre and tiara, Prelates of the Segna-tura carrying seven candles and a Prelate of the Rota bearing the papal cross, the Latin subdeacon between the deacon and subdeacon of the Greek rite, the penitentiaries of St. Peter's who carry as a symbol of their powers two long, slender wands which are now adorned with gaily coloured flowers. Attention is next seized by the choir of the papal *Cappella,* singing as they follow their choir-master, who conducts them while walking backwards, with his arms above his head. Next come, in the order of their precedence in the hierarchy, wearing white mitres, the abbots, bishops, archbishops and patriarchs, with the beard-ed representatives of the Eastern Church among them. Behind these come the College of Cardinals, also wearing white mitres: the Cardinal Deacons in dalmatics, the Cardi-nal Priests in chasubles and the Cardinal Bishops vested like the other archbishops and bishops. After the Dean of the Sacred College, after the commanding officers of the Swiss Guard and the Palatine Guard and other dignitaries, comes the Pope himself, carried on the *sedia gestatoria* which rests upon the shoulders of bearers dressed in damask livery. Above the Pope a silken canopy is held, and on either side of him the two *flabella,* great fans made of ostrich feathers. The Holy Father wears a red or white cope, embroidered in gold, and on his head is the tiara. The *sedia gestatoria* is escorted by officers of the Noble Guard, in their bright red tunics and ceremonial helmets, and of the Swiss Guard. Following one may see the lay Privy Chamberlains Participating *di spada e cappa* in their Spanish court dress with cloaks and swords and white ruffs, and, after them, more senior prelates of the Pontifical Court. Storms of applause, waved handkerchiefs

11

and cries of acclamation break loose everywhere as the Pope passes. This is the moment when the Church displays the wealth of her tradition, the magnificence of her colour, the immense attraction of her majestic dignity and the always significant splendour of her external appearances.

The pilgrim to Rome will carry this moment in his memory for the rest of his life; but it is only one moment in the life of the Church. The mysterious currents of religious life which the Church guards at their sources and which she directs by divine command throughout the whole world provide everywhere the same means of salvation and grace: in the splendour of St. Peter's and in the simple village church, in the newest churches of great modern cities and in the tents of missionaries at the edge of the desert. Everywhere where believers gather in the communion of the faith, there is the Church. But the Church is not only a communion of the faith; she is also a communion of the law; a communion of men who need guidance, order, administration and organization. Rome is the central point of that worldwide organization and discipline. A visible reflection of it is unfolded before the eyes of those who are present in Rome on the great feast-days, when the glory of the Church is manifested in rich ceremonies; but the everyday life of Rome has a different appearance, a different style, a different rhythm. On feast-days Rome shines in splendour; on ordinary days Rome works. The Church is governed on ordinary days. In studies and offices, amid documents and filing-systems, telephones and telegrams and wireless communication, by means of the spoken and the printed word, the greatest system of government in the world is carried on.

Who knows what makes this vast machinery work? There is a secret about that. But let not that word lead the reader to think of the secrets of sealed documents or of the official secrets of the service of the Church. Let him think instead of the profound secret of the existence of the Church. The Church is not of this world and yet is in this world. She has an eternal mission in a world that is transient. She is unchanging in her religious essence and at the same time changes in her historical appearance. She is a divinely-founded institution to which has been given the promise that the gates of hell shall not prevail against her. She is at the same time a perishable work of the human hands which shaped her visible form. She is the Mystical Body of Christ and at the same time a juridically formed and organized community of men. The history of the Church teaches how a divine purpose is achieved through human means and prevails over human weakness; how the

13

eternal is associated with the temporal without becoming lost in it; how all that is essential is consistently preserved through all temporal changes. Out of the eternal and the temporal is also wrought the secret of the central administration and organization of the Church – the Roman Curia.

The following chapters give some detailed information about the Roman Curia. The essentials of the subject-matter of these pages can be found in any text-book of canon law. The intention of the present writer is only to seek to convey such understanding as he has himself acquired in Rome, amplified by further reading, and to do so in a clear and easily understandable way. In describing "How the Church is Governed" he has deliberately restricted himself to the central institutions of the Church – the Papacy, the Cardinals and the Curia. He has not attempted any description of the Vatican City State as it was constituted by the Lateran agreements of 1929, nor of the local government of the Church in dioceses throughout the world.

1

THE POPE AND THE CARDINALS

THE PLENITUDE OF POWER

THE Roman Curia is the collective term for all the ecclesiastical offices through which the Pope, endowed with the *plenitudo potestatis,* the plenitude of the power of his primacy, governs the Church in the communion of faith, practice and law. The present form of the Curia and its manner of working date from the great reforms which St. Pius X introduced on June 29, 1908, with the Apostolic Constitution *Sapienti Consilio,* the substance of which was afterwards incorporated in the new Code of Canon Law published in 1917. But only by considering its long historical development can its hierarchical structure and the distribution of its powers be understood.

The word "development" here has a particular meaning. The history of the Roman Curia is one of progressive centralization. That does not mean, however, that in the course of history the central power of the Papacy has acquired anything which was not implicitly there before. In a process of constant change and growth resulting from

15

the changing requirements of the times it has developed new structural lines, new forms, new organs, without essentially gaining anything. There has been no acquisition of new power, only historical development and the expansion of powers which essentially and implicitly had always been contained within the papal primacy. As the successor of St. Peter and the vicar of Christ on earth the Pope possessed this plenitude of power from the beginning. Just as the spreading branches of a tree have grown from a small seed which held all this potential growth latent within it, so has the Papacy, in possession of this central authority from the beginning gradually and with changing times given effect to that authority. Whereas during the first centuries the Popes only intervened in particular cases in the administration of the Church as a whole, and gave only at the request of the bishops the decisions out of which the rules of canon law later developed, in later years the power of the bishops became limited by this process, so that matters by nature of particular importance and moment came by right of law under the jurisdiction and the active and permanent control of the central papal power. At first the Pope chose his advisers in the government of the Church from among the Roman clergy, but as time went on and the work of government became more complicated, certain

16

When he is wearing his imposing ceremonial robes –
which were simplified by order of Pius XII – a Cardinal
appears in the full splendour of the purple; and here it
ought perhaps to be added that the Cardinal's purple, as it
is generally called, is not really purple at all, but scarlet.
The cassock and broad sash over which a rochet of white
lace is worn are scarlet; also scarlet are the knee-length
sleeveless mantelletta and the cape, known as a mozetta,
which is worn round the shoulders; the cappa magna is
scarlet, as is the wide hooded cloak which in winter is
trimmed with ermine and which used to be so long
that in the days when their Eminences still went about
on horseback it enveloped both horse and rider. During
Advent and Lent, or when the Pope has died and his
successor has not yet been elected, and on certain other
occasions, the Cardinals wear violet instead of scarlet.
Those Cardinals who are members of religious Orders
usually wear the colour of the habit of their Order, but
all Cardinals wear a scarlet skull-cap and biretta. Their
full ceremonial dress, however, is prescribed only for
rare ceremonial occasions, at which each Cardinal must
be attended by a *gentiluomo* wearing the court dress of the
Spanish monarchy. For everyday wear a Cardinal has
a black cassock with a short cape round his shoulders,
with scarlet piping, scarlet buttons and a broad scarlet

sash; with this goes the flat black hat worn by all the Roman clergy, but carrying a red and golden cord. When he is paying official visits he wears a *ferraiolone* of scarlet silk. In winter he wears a heavy, full-length cloak of violet or scarlet, with a collar of gold braid or scarlet velvet. But when he goes on foot through the streets of Rome a Cardinal is only to be identified by the expert bystander.

If a Cardinal's quarters, where he lives, are furnished according to the traditional prescriptions, they include an ante-room with a little table draped in scarlet velvet above which the Cardinal's coat-of-arms hangs beneath a canopy; a biretta-room, in which the biretta lies on a little table before a crucifix; and a throne-room, where the walls and the gilt chairs are covered in scarlet damask, and where a portrait of the reigning Pope hangs beneath a canopy and above the throne on which the Pope would sit if he should call upon the Cardinal in the Cardinal's residence. So that no unauthorized person shall sit upon it, the throne is usually turned towards the wall. Adjoining the reception rooms are the Cardinal's private apartments, which include a private chapel. All these prescriptions – nowadays no longer obligatory – date from a time when the purple was worn almost exclusively by the sons of great and wealthy families. Today most Cardinals would for financial reasons alone find it difficult to observe all the rules of etiquette. Certainly the *piatto,* the stipend of a curial Cardinal, would not suffice.[1] The Cardinal Datary and the Cardinal who is Chancellor of the Holy Roman Church usually live in their office buildings, and the others live in private quarters in the city of Rome. Only the Cardinal Secretary of State lives in the Vatican.

[1] The stipend was substantially increased, as were the wages or stipends of all those working at the Vatican, from the highest to the humblest, by Pope John XXIII in the summer of 1959.

Translator

2

THE CONSISTORY

The Secret Consistory

The creation of Cardinals takes place in the consistory which is still summoned today, twice a year or less frequently, mainly for this reason or at the conclusion of a canonization process. If the reason is the creation of new Cardinals, to take one of these two reasons as an example, the first step is the summoning of a secret consistory, which traditionally takes place on a Monday. At the appointed hour the Pope comes with his attendants from his apartments to the Consistorial Hall of the Vatican. There all the Cardinals have already assembled. The first word comes from the Master of Ceremonies: *Extra omnes,* he cries; "All outside". Thereupon the Pontifical Court withdraws: the Major-domo, the prelates in attendance, the chamberlains, the Noble Guard. Attendants in liveries of scarlet silk carefully close the doors, for in the secret consistory the Pope is alone with the Cardinals. The Pope sits on a raised throne under a canopy; the Cardinals sit to left and right along the tapestried walls.

The Pope opens the consistory with an address, which, either in part or in whole, is usually released for publication afterwards. Often it surveys the most pressing concerns of the government of the Church; or it selects one particular important event; or it develops the general lines of policy concerning the world and the Church. When this is finished there are usually several other items on the agenda to be dealt with: the annual appointment of the camerlengo of the Sacred College, the appointment of the chancellor and the camerlengo of the Holy Roman Church if these positions should have fallen vacant through the death of their previous occupants, the assignment of the pallium, the symbol of the highest episcopal authority, to newly-appointed Patriarchs, Metropolitan archbishops and certain bishops, and, finally, the reading of the list of all archbishops and bishops appointed since the last consistory. But before this the Pope announces the names of those whom he wishes to make Cardinals. *Quid vobis videtur?* he then enquires; and the question recalls the time when it was for the consistory to resolve and decide; "What do you think?" Each Cardinal rises, gathers up his cappa magna, the scarlet hooded cloak, removes his skullcap and silently bows his head in token of assent. Then the Pope utters the words of appointment: "By the authority of Almighty God, of

37

the Holy Apostles Peter and Paul and of our self, we appoint to be Cardinals . . . . In the name of the Father and of the Son and of the Holy Ghost, Amen." Sometimes he adds another sentence: "To these we add a Cardinal (or two, or more) whom we reserve in our breast" – in Latin, *in pectore,* and in Italian, *in petto* – "and whom we will make known when we deem it opportune."

Those so designated are known as Cardinals reserved *in petto;* nobody knows their names except the Pope, and even if their names became known they could claim no rights or titles as Cardinals. If the Pope dies without having formally made known the names of the Cardinals *in petto* nothing more is heard about them. If their names are mentioned in the Pope's will his successor is in no way bound by the fact. If, however, the name of a Cardinal *in petto* is published by the Pope at a later consistory, then the seniority of such a Cardinal is dated retrospectively from the day when he was reserved *in petto*. It has sometimes happened in the past that a Cardinal's stipend has been claimed retrospectively in such cases; sometimes, indeed, the reason for a reservation *in petto* has been that the Pope has wanted, by ensuring the payment of an accumulated retrospective stipend, to ease the considerable financial outlay which a Cardinal has to make when he receives the red hat. But all this has been changed by the new Code of Canon Law, which restricts retrospective claims to seniority. A well-known case of a Cardinal reserved *in petto* was that of Cardinal Bertram, the last German Archbishop of Breslau, who died in 1945; he was reserved *in petto* by Pope Benedict XV in a consistory on December 4, 1916, but was not publicly announced as a Cardinal until three years later, when the first world war was over. The reason for that reservation *in petto* was that the Pope was anxious to bestow the dignity of a Cardinal upon the archbishop and yet on the other hand did not want to take any step which might in time of war have been interpreted as a political gesture. In other cases it may be that the Pope wishes to reward a prelate who has given good service in the Curia or in the diplomatic service of the Holy See and yet cannot spare him in his present position and work. The reservation *in petto* makes it possible to do what is best from both points of view.

THE SEMI-PUBLIC AND PUBLIC CONSISTORIES

A Cardinal receives all his rights and attributes at the time of his appointment in the secret consistory. Meanwhile, however, various ceremonies follow, in which he is solemnly invested with the insignia of his dignity.

Immediately after the secret consistory papal messengers call upon those of the newly appointed Princes of the

Church who are present in Rome, to deliver the *biglietti,* the written news of their elevation to the purple. Thereupon prelates, diplomats and friends of each new Cardinal call upon him, paying the congratulatory visits known as the visits *di calore.* Usually on the Wednesday afternoon following, in the presence of distinguished guests who have assembled in the Consistorial Hall, the Pope, after delivering an address, places the biretta on the heads of the new Cardinals. He then receives them in private audience, after which each is handed the scarlet skullcap by an attendant. Those newly-appointed Cardinals who are serving away from Rome as Nuncios in some cases do not return for the public consistory; instead, a small delegation is despatched, usually consisting of a prelate as *Ablegatus* and a member of the Noble Guard; the same procedure used sometimes to be followed in the past with residential archbishops and bishops raised to the Sacred College. The member of the Noble Guard goes first and presents the scarlet skull-cap to the new Cardinal; later the *Ablegatus* follows with the biretta which, by a tradition followed in some countries, is conferred upon the new Cardinal by the Head of the State. It was so in 1953 that the future Pope John XXIII received his scarlet biretta as a Cardinal from the Socialist President of the French Republic, M. Vincent Auriol.

The secret consistory having taken place on a Monday, the public consistory, with the imposition of the *galero,* the time-honoured red hat, normally takes place on the Thursday of the same week. Not only the Pope and the Cardinals take part in this public consistory, but also archbishops and bishops, many members of the Pontifical Court, members of the diplomatic corps accredited to the Holy See, and, in a limited number, guests also. The new Cardinals have previously visited the Sistine Chapel, where they have taken the oath of allegiance before the Deans of the three orders of Cardinals, the Cardinal Bishops, the Cardinal Priests and the Cardinal Deacons, and before the Cardinal Camerlengo. They are then conducted into the consistory, which on this occasion usually meets in the Sala della Benedizione, above the portico of St. Peter's. There the time has been filled with historical reminders of the powerful position which the consistory held in the past. The secretary of the Congregation of Rites and the consistorial advocates have taken their places before the papal throne, and one of the advocates has begun to read a petition based upon the findings of a process of canonization. The reading is interrupted when the new *purpurati* enter the hall. They pay homage to the Pope, receiving the kiss of peace which they pass on to the old Cardinals. Then they return to the steps of the throne, and the Pope places the traditional red hat on the head of each, saying these words as he does so: "Receive this symbol of the dignity of the cardinalate, which signifies that you must show yourself intrepid for the exaltation of the Holy Faith, the peace and tranquility of Christian peoples and the conservation and growth of the Holy Roman Church, even if need be to the shedding of your blood."

The red hat (its colour and that of the robes of a Cardinal is symbolical of the words with which it is imposed) is quite flat in shape, with a broad circular brim from which hang two silken cords with, in all, thirty tassels. In the past it used to be worn on solemn occasions on the hood of the cappa magna, but by present custom it touches the head of the Cardinal only on this one occasion of the imposition in the public consistory. It only appears again when the Cardinal has died, when it rests at the foot of the body during the lying in state, and then on the coffin, finally being hung in the church above the tomb.

With the imposition of the red hat the public consistory closes, but another secret consistory follows. In this the Pope carries out the traditional ceremony of opening and closing the mouths of the new Cardinals. The closing of the mouth symbolizes a kind of novitiate for the Cardinals; in recollected silence they are to prepare themselves for their exalted task. A little later the mouth is opened again; they are symbolically called to the power and authority of their office, each being charged "to give your opinions in consistories, in congregations and in other cardinalatial functions". The Pope then gives each the Cardinal's ring, and bestows the title of a church upon each Cardinal Priest and the title of a deaconry on each Cardinal Deacon. With this the secret consistory closes.

CONSISTORIES FOR OTHER PURPOSES

When the consistory is summoned not for the purpose of appointing Cardinals but as the last act in a process for canonization which has already passed through the Congregation of Rites, then a secret, a public and a semi-public consistory are convened in succession. In the secret consistory the Cardinal Prefect of the Congregation of Rites reports on the course of the process hitherto and the Cardinals cast a preliminary vote in the order of their seniority. In the public consistory the consistorial advocates plead for the completion of the canonization and the Pope informs the Cardinals through one of the prelates of his court, the Secretary of Briefs to Princes, that he wishes to hear the opinion of the bishops before taking a final decision; and this he does in the semi–public consistory, to which are invited, in addition to the Cardinals, those archbishops and bishops who live within a distance of approximately sixty two miles from Rome. But this expression of the opinion of the bishops is also only a formality. By the time this semi-public consistory is called the date for the canonization has usually already been settled, and the decisive and final judgment has already been reached, that the canonization can now be proceeded with "in safety".

3

THE CONCLAVE

The Death of the Pope

ONLY on one occasion does the College of Cardinals assume the same decisive power and influence that it held in the past, and that is when, following the death of a Pope, it exercises the most exalted, important and exclusive of its rights in the election of the new Pope. With the death of the Pope a peculiar change takes place in the legal structure of the monarchically governed Church. The wheels of the Curial machinery have come to a standstill. The fisherman's ring of the Pope and the great seal are broken. The offices of the Cardinal Secretary of State and the Cardinal Datary have ceased to exist. Only the Cardinal Grand Penitentiary, the Cardinal Chancellor, the Cardinal Vicar and his Vicegerent who administer the diocese of Rome, and the papal Almoner remain in office, so that consciences, pastoral care and the poor shall not suffer from the death of the Pope. The pontifical power is in abeyance. Nor is it temporarily transferred to the College of Cardinals; it would be truer to say that the College of Cardinals fills the position of a trustee, with clearly defined tasks. It has to safeguard and defend the rights of the Papacy without itself encroaching upon them. Matters of minor importance, if they are urgent, go through the normal administrative channels. Whatever can be deferred is deferred. Important decisions which cannot be delayed have to come before the plenary assembly of the Cardinals; but the decisions there reached are only provisional in character and are formulated in such a way that the future Pope is not deprived of the freedom to alter or revoke them. In addition, it falls to the College of Cardinals to make the arrangements for the obsequies of the dead Pope and the preparations for the election of his successor.

The Camerlengo

The most important figure in the days of the *sede vacante,* the vacancy of the Holy See, is the Cardinal Camerlengo. During the lifetime of the Pope the Camerlengo holds a nominal position rather than an office. But now he stands at the head of the College of Cardinals. His first duty is to confirm the death of the Pope officially. He draws back the white cloth which covers the face of the Pope on the death-bed and calls him three times by his Christian names. (There is no truth in the old legend that he taps three times upon the forehead of the dead Pope with a silver or ivory hammer). Then he utters the words, "The Pope is indeed dead." From this moment onwards the Camerlengo, who hardly leaves the Vatican until the opening of the Conclave, is accompanied by an escort of the Swiss Guard. It now falls to him to convene, prepare and conduct the daily meetings of the Cardinals, the so-called General Congregation, in which those of them who are resident in Rome are joined by the daily arrival of Cardinals from all parts of the world.

The rules governing the election of the Pope are read at the first General Congregation, and the Cardinals take an oath at the hands of the Camerlengo – those arriving later must take the oath at a later meeting – swearing to pay the most careful attention to the rules and conditions of the election; above all not to let themselves become the tools of temporal powers seeking to interfere in the election of the Pope; to maintain a strict secrecy about the proceedings in the Conclave; and, in the event of their own election, not to relinquish the temporal rights of the Apostolic See which safeguard the freedom and independence of the Papacy. Nowadays the Cardinals have also to swear that they will not use any wireless, telephones, microphones or other receiving or transmitting apparatus, or make use of cameras or cine-cameras during the conclave.

47

On an appointed day the General Congregation receives the diplomatic corps, whose members all come together to express condolences on the death of the Pope. After this the College of Cardinals is not allowed to receive visits from individual diplomats. Since the Cardinal Secretary of State is no longer in office, the secretary of the College of Cardinals has to keep in touch with the various diplomatic missions of the Holy See. Any reports from Nuncios that are of special importance, and all telegrams of condolence, pass through his hands before being placed before the Camerlengo and the General Congregation, in which any major decisions are taken by a secret majority vote. For the conduct of day-to-day affairs and decisions of minor importance the Camerlengo has at his disposal a commission of three Cardinals, the senior members of the three orders of Cardinals who are replaced every three days by the next in seniority, forming with the Camerlengo what is known as the particular congregation.

THE OBSEQUIES

Meanwhile, on the instructions of the General Congregation, the obsequies of the dead Pope have begun. From the room in which he died the body has been brought to the Sistine Chapel, where it lies dressed in white, with a scarlet ermine-trimmed mozzetta. For two days the penitentiaries of St. Peter's keep watch by the dead Pope by the light of tall candles. In the evening of the third day the body is vested in pontifical vestments and, in solemn procession, is carried into St. Peter's, where it lies in state in the chapel of the Blessed Sacrament. All through the next day the people of Rome file past the gates of the chapel, and the following evening the doors of St. Peter's are closed to the public. From the Chapel of the Blessed Sacrament in the aisle on the epistle side the canons of St. Peter's escort the body of the Pope over to the gospel side of the great basilica, into the Chapel of the Choir, where it is placed in a coffin of cypress-wood. This is sealed and placed within a leaden coffin, which in turn is sealed and placed within a coffin of elm. By the gentle light of the candles and the sombre light of the torches the triple-sealed coffin is then temporarily laid in a niche in the wall near the Chapel of the Choir, whence later on it is finally taken to the crypt of St. Peter's or to another Roman church. Henceforward an empty cata-falque is erected for the solemn Requiem Masses which are celebrated on nine consecutive days in St. Peter's and in the Sistine Chapel. The last three of these Requiem Masses are celebrated with particular solemnity, and a Latin eulogy is delivered at the last of them.

The Pope is dead. The Cardinals must turn their minds to the election of a new Pope. The conclave can begin.

The Electoral Assembly

The three fundamental conditions of the election of the Pope – election by the Cardinals, the two-thirds majority, and the conclave – were developed in the Middle Ages as a protection against irregularities and encroachments of the temporal powers. In the earlier periods of Church history the Pope was elected, as were all other bishops, by the clergy and people of his diocese, amongst whom there arose electoral factions, in which temporal influence and arbitrary interventions became rampant. First the Roman Emperors in the West and after their fall the Germanic military Kings, then the Byzantine Emperors, the Franconian Kings and the German Emperors, all exercised a powerful influence in the choice of an occupant of the Apostolic See. Only gradually did the Church succeed in freeing herself from the temporal grasp and in establishing her own laws for the election of the Pope; but even this could not wholly prevent temporal powers from exerting their influence as the result of human weakness and the compelling force of events. In the year 1059 Pope Nicholas II reserved the right to elect the Pope for the Cardinal Bishops. In 1179 Alexander III, while giving cathedral chapters the right to elect bishops, gave the right of electing the Pope to all the orders of Cardinals, and at the same time introduced the rule of the two-thirds majority. Pius XII altered this latter rule in one important point when he redefined the laws governing the election of the Pope, in the Apostolic Constitution *Vacantis Apostolicae Sedis* of December 8, 1945; since then an election, to be valid, has required a majority of two-thirds plus one. The earlier rule by which a vote cast by any candidate for himself was invalid lost its practical meaning thereby. If the secrecy of the ballot was to be safeguarded it could only be ensured by a system of voting as complicated as it was ingeniously devised. The new rule automatically prevents a two-thirds majority being brought about by a candidate voting for himself.

But what if the Cardinals should be unable to reach agreement? This frequently happened in the thirteenth century, when the *sede vacante* periods became longer and longer and did more and more harm to the Church. The situation became intolerable after the death of Clement IV in November 1268, when the See of Peter remained neglected for nearly three years. Eighteen Cardinals who met at Viterbo were unable to come to an agreement. The people of Viterbo then resorted to a drastic measure which had earlier in the same century been applied in Rome and in Naples; they walled up the entrance to the Episcopal Palace in which the Cardinals were assembled. When this brought no result they took off the roof, to expose the Cardinals to the weather, and deprived them of all food save bread and water. So it was that Gregory X was elected, on September 1, 1271. The new Pope made a law out of the drastic plan which the people of Viterbo had devised; since that time the Popes have been elected in a conclave, and the word "conclave", from the Latin word *conclave,* meaning a room which can be locked, denotes the actual sealed chamber in which the election takes place as well as the electoral assembly of the Cardinals. In the beginning the rules were very strict; all the Cardinals had to live together in one room, and their meals, which after three days consisted of only one dish and after a week consisted of bread and water alone, with a little wine, were passed in to them through a window. Later on these rules were somewhat modified, but the strict seclusion of the electoral assembly from the outside world is to this day the essential characteristic of the conclave, and it has today the same purpose that it had then: to make any external influence impossible, and to make the election as rapid as possible.

The preparations for the election begin, under the direction of the General Congregation, soon after the death of the Pope. Part of the Vatican Palace, if that is where the election is to take place – and in theory it can take place anywhere in the world – is so arranged that every means of access to the outside world is either cut off or brought under trustworthy and rigorous control. Doors and corridors leading from the conclave are barred or walled up, and any remaining access is closely guarded. The windows are curtained and sealed. Letters have to pass through a censorship, and the telephone cannot be used directly; if any telephone calls have to be made the message has to be written down and passed on by a third person. A number of large rooms have been partitioned off, so that each Cardinal can have a small apartment of his own, the allocation of these being decided by lot. Each Cardinal can have two attendants with him in the conclave, clerics or laymen, or one of each; usually a secretary and a servant.

The most recent regulations stipulate that if possible only one of the two shall be a layman. Prelates and kinsmen of the Cardinals are not admitted to the conclave. A Cardinal who is a member of a religious order is not permitted to have a member of the same order with him. Others who enter the conclave are the sacristan of the Apostolic Palace; up to six Masters of Ceremonies; the secretary of the College of Cardinals; one member of a religious Order to serve as confessor; two physicians, one surgeon and one dispensing chemist with his assistant; and such others as the General Congregation may deem necessary. The Marshal of the Conclave is responsible for external order within the conclave, and this office is traditionally reserved to the family of Prince Chigi, who has a college of senior prelates to advise him.

The Election of the Pope

The conclave must begin at least fifteen days and not more than eighteen days after the death of a Pope. (That is the normal course of events, but the Holy See can also in theory become vacant through voluntary resignation, madness or the private heresy of the Pope). This period that elapses before the conclave opens was reduced by Pius X, but soon after the election of Pius XI the rule was changed and the period extended to what it is today, as a result of what happened at the election of Pius XI in 1922, when the ten-day rule that was then in force made it impossible for the American Cardinals to reach Rome in time. Today, of course, it would be quite easy for the American Cardinals to arrive by air within ten days. In the morning of the sixteenth day after the death of the Pope, or at the latest in the morning of the nineteenth day, the Dean of the Sacred College celebrates a Mass of the

Holy Ghost before the assembled Cardinals; a senior prelate of the Pontifical Court delivers a Latin oration about the duties of the Cardinals as the electors of the Pope and, either immediately afterwards or in the evening of the same day, the Cardinals and their *conclavisti* go in solemn procession to the Sistine Chapel. There the regulations governing the election are read aloud once more – that is, the Apostolic Constitution of Pius XII, *Vacantis Apostolicae Sedis,* dated December 8, 1945, which we have already mentioned. The Cardinals and all those entitled to enter the conclave swear that they will obey the laws there laid down. After this a bell is rung three times, the Masters of Ceremonies cry *Extra omnes,* and all those who are not entering the conclave depart. The doors are closed; the Camerlengo and the Cardinals from the three orders who with him form the Particular Congregation make a tour of the conclave area to make sure that all instructions have been carried out and that no unauthorized persons have remained behind; and the conclave is sealed.

The following morning, after a Mass of the Holy Ghost celebrated by the Cardinal Dean at which those Cardinals who are not themselves celebrating Mass receive Holy Communion, and after the singing of the *Veni Creator,* the election begins. This may take place in three ways: as it were by divine inspiration *(quasi per inspirationem);* by

55

compromise *(per compromissum)*; and by voting by ballot *(per scrutinium)*. The first two forms occur only rarely and by way of exception, and can only occur if all the Cardinals agree. In the first case, *quasi per inspirationem,* the procedure roughly corresponds to the method of election by acclamation that is sometimes found in temporal affairs: one Cardinal makes a proposal, all the others agree, none raises any objection. In the second case, *per compromissum,* the Cardinals unanimously delegate the right of voting to a commission chosen from among themselves. The method usually employed, however, is that of election *per scrutinium,* the secret election by ballot, in which all the details of the procedure are minutely laid down by law.

If the conclave takes place at the Vatican the election is held in the Sistine Chapel. Before the altar stands a table on which is the voting-urn, in the form of a large golden chalice. Along the length of the walls on either side are the thrones of the Cardinals, with a little canopy above each. Before each of these stands a little table with paper and pen, sealing-wax and a candle. In the middle are several larger tables at which the scrutiny of the votes takes place. The Masters of Ceremonies distribute the ballot-papers, and the Cardinals are then left alone in the chapel. They proceed to appoint three Cardinals by lot to serve as scrutineers, three to check the result of the scrutiny, and three more whose duty it is to collect the ballot-papers from those Cardinals who are infirm and cannot walk to the urn.

The wording and form of the ballot-paper are also specified in detail by the law governing the conclave. On the obverse side are two panels. In the upper panel are written the words, *Eligo in Summum Pontificem Rev.mum* – either printed or written in each case in the same hand-writing. In the lower panel the Cardinal writes the name of whomever he wishes to elect as Pope, doing so in a disguised handwriting so as not to reveal his identity. The ballot-paper therefore looks like this:

Eligo in Summum Pontificem Rev.mum

— — — — — — — —

D. meum D. Card.

It is folded in the middle, so that it becomes a long slip.

When the ballot-papers have been filled in for the first time the Cardinals walk to the urn in the order of their seniority. Each kneels for a short prayer before the altar, and after the oath, "I take Christ the Lord Who will judge me as my witness that I shall elect him whom before God I believe I ought to elect", he lets the slip fall from the paten into the chalice. The ballot-papers of those Cardinals who are confined to their rooms because of illness are collected in a special urn. The counting and scrutiny of the votes then begins at the table in the middle. If at one ballot no Cardinal has received the necessary majority of two thirds plus one, another ballot follows immediately. If this ballot also is unsuccessful the ballot-papers are burned in a stove with wet hay or straw. The black smoke which then rises from the chimney of the Sistine Chapel tells the waiting crowd in St. Peter's Square that these ballots have brought no result. In the afternoon of the same day two more ballots are taken; and so it continues, with four ballots each day until the necessary majority of two-thirds plus one has been achieved. When the correct majority has been reached the ballot-papers are burned without the addition of hay or straw; and when the smoke then rises outside in thin white puffs the people know: *Habemus Papam,* We have a Pope.

Inside the Sistine Chapel the Cardinals have pulled the cords which roll back the canopies above each place. Only one canopy remains as it was before, that of the newly-elected Pope. The Cardinal Dean approaches him and asks him whether he will accept election, and at the moment of acceptance he who has been elected receives the plenitude of the papal power. He is then asked what name he will take. To his answer the new Pope usually adds a brief account of his reasons for the choice. Then he is robed in one of the three white cassocks which, in different sizes, have been prepared in advance, and for the first time he receives the homage of the Cardinals. Meanwhile the senior Cardinal Deacon has appeared on the loggia above the central doors of St. Peter's and has announced to the people, *Annuntio vobis gaudium magnum. . . .*: "I bring you tidings of great joy; we have a Pope, the Most Eminent and Most Reverend Lord Cardinal . . . who has taken the name of. . . ." Soon after this the new Pope himself appears on the loggia – a custom reintroduced by Pius XI – to give the papal blessing *urbi et orbi,* to the city and the world.

If the new Pope should be not yet a priest or a bishop – which in theory is possible, since there is no law which lays down any such condition for the election of a Pope – then it would be the duty of the Cardinal Dean to ordain and consecrate him. But with only one exception since the end of the thirteenth century only Cardinals have in fact been elected as Popes. The wording on the ballot-paper, as we have just seen, assumes that votes will be cast only for Cardinals. And under the Code of Canon Law it is now stipulated that every Cardinal shall be a priest, although he need not be a bishop.

59

The coronation of the Pope, at which the senior Cardinal Deacon places the triple crown, the tiara, symbol of the three-fold papal power, on the head of the Pope, whose reign is officially reckoned from this day, is no more than a ceremony, adding nothing to the rights and power which the Pope holds. As he places the tiara on the Pope's head the senior Cardinal Deacon says, "Receive the tiara with the three crowns, and know that thou art the father of kings and princes, the pastor of the universe and the Vicar on earth of our Lord Jesus Christ, to Whom be honour and glory, world without end, Amen." Earlier, at the solemn entry to the coronation Mass, the Pope has been met by a Master of Ceremonies bearing a gilded staff at the end of which pieces of tow are burning, who, as the flame flares and dies again, slowly speaks these words: *"Sancte pater, sic transit gloria mundi"*, "Holy Father, so passes the glory of the world."

4

THE ROMAN CONGREGATIONS

AMONG those organs of the Roman Curia which were formed with the passage of time out of the plenary assembly of the Cardinals in the consistory, congregations, offices, tribunals and commissions are to be found. The juridical foundations of the present-day structure of the Curia date from the great reform which St. Pius X carried out with the Apostolic Constitution *Sapienti Consilio* of June 29, 1908, the essentials of which were incorporated in the new Code of Canon Law promulgated in 1917.

The congregations are corporately organized central authorities which may be regarded as the ministries of the Church. Each has its own special competence under the authority of the Pope. In the structure of each congregation one may distinguish between an executive body, which consists exclusively of Cardinals, and an associated administrative body in which the preliminary work is done before a decision. In three congregations, the Holy Office, the Consistorial Congregation and that for the

Eastern Church, the Pope himself is head of the executive body; in each of the others that office is held by a Cardinal, who is known as its Prefect. At the head of the administrative body is a secretary (with an under-secretary), an office which is held by a senior prelate, sometimes an archbishop or bishop. When the Pope himself is Prefect, however, the duties of a secretary devolve upon a Cardinal, who in this case is assisted in the administrative work by an assessor and a deputy or *sostituto*. The secretary or the assessor is in practice the effective head of the administration, and he, like all the other higher officials of a congregation so far mentioned, is appointed by the Pope himself. Appointments of the lower officials are made after candidates have passed certain examinations, or on the special recommendation of the Prefect. These include in particular, apart from the necessary secretarial staff, the experts, known as *minutanti,* who usually hold triple doctorates, in theology and in both canon and civil law, and who, apart from Latin and Italian, have to speak at least one other language – either French or German, English, Spanish or Portuguese. (The stipends paid to officials of the Curia, incidentally, are very low, and bear no comparison with the salaries paid to those who hold comparable positions in civil life.) The advisers or consultors attached to the congregations are not necessarily resident in Rome, but are called upon in their advisory capacity as the need arises. Matters of minor importance are dealt with in a conference *(congressus)* attended by the Prefect, the secretary and the closest assistants of the secretary. More important questions are brought before the plenary assembly of the congregation and, with the Prefect presiding, are decided by a majority vote. One of the Cardinals of the congregation serves on these occasions as *rapporteur*.

The decisions of the congregations are usually given in concise Latin formulas. They answer a carefully worded question previously agreed upon by those concerned, and consist simply of the words *affirmative, negative* or *dilata* (postponed) as the case may be – to cite only the most frequent formulas of the official style of the Curia. When a dossier carries the marginal note *lectum* (read), it means that no answer will be given – without necessarily implying that the absence of an answer is itself an answer. When necessary an explanation is added to the decision of a congregation. Unless the Pope has expressly delegated matters of minor importance to be settled in the course of day-to-day business, all decisions of the congregation need his personal assent. They are submitted to him in the audiences which he grants to the Prefect and the secretary, the so-called audiences *di tabella* which take place regularly on certain days at certain hours. He is not bound by a decision of the congregation, but can confirm, vary or reject it. If the confirmation (or variation) is given "in the usual form" then the decision is still legally not the Pope's but the congregation's – that is, it can be revoked or varied later on, and is not generally binding but only in the particular case for which the decision was made. If a generally binding law is to be established as the result of a decision, then the Pope must confirm it "in special form". But it should be added that such decisions, unless they are dogmatic utterances, are only infallible in character if the Pope expressly makes them so under the necessary conditions. Only in that case are such decisions final.

Decisions which are considered to be of public interest are published in the Curia's official gazette, the *Acta Apostolicae Sedis*. Anyone anxious to expedite his business at the Curia may avail himself of the services of so-called agents or procurators whose names are entered in an official list, inclusion in the list being the condition of acceptability. For example, the agents of the German bishops in their dealings with the Curia are the rectors of the seminaries attached to the German national church of Santa Maria dell' Anima and the rector of the Collegio Teutonico di Santa Maria in Campo Santo, which specializes in the archaeology and history of the Church. Advocates are similarly admitted in the tribunals of the Curia.

THE HOLY OFFICE

Pre-eminent among all the congregations is the most important and oldest of them, the Supreme Sacred Congregation of the Holy Office, which was established in 1542 as the supreme tribunal of the inquisition. Its name refers to the sacred duty of protecting and safeguarding the faith and morals of the Church against any false teaching. It is charged to teach and to exercise vigilance, and is a tribunal at the same time, with jurisdiction wherever heresy is concerned. Its competence embraces the whole world and all the faithful, whether they come from the Latin Church, the Eastern Church or the mission territories. It is in effect the central point in the worldwide power of the Church. The impressive unity of belief and teaching within the Church finds in the Holy Office an expression as magnificent as it is unyielding. The Pope himself is the Prefect of this congregation, and to be a member of it is a high distinction. The tremendous importance which is thus bestowed on it accounts for the strict secrecy which surrounds its proceedings and the oath by which all who take part in its work are bound to that secrecy. Anyone violating the oath and the secrecy is *ipso facto* excluded from the Church, and can only be reconciled by the Pope personally. The once independent congregation of the Index was made part of the Holy Office by Benedict XV in 1917, and now forms a separate department of it, watching over publications and the reading of books that are contrary to faith and morals, and keeping, not very systematically, the Index of Forbidden Works, *Index librorum prohibitorum* – a method of carrying out its duty which gives rise to a good deal of controversy inside as well as outside the Church. There is also the *Index Expurgatorius,* a list of passages expunged from certain books which may then be freely read.

The secretary of the Holy Office is a Cardinal, and the leading officials in its administration are the *assessore* and the *commissario;* the latter, with his two assistants, belongs to the Order of Preachers, and it is his task to initiate penal processes. The officials of the Holy Office also include consultors, notaries and *qualificatori;* the latter so-called because they have to determine the degree and quality of a heresy. In cases coming before the tribunal there is an official prosecutor *(promotore di giustizia,* or, in Latin, *promotor iustitiae)* and an official advocate for the defence *(avvocato dei rei,* or *advocatus reorum).* The plenary assembly of the congregation meets every Wednesday; the assessor has an audience with the Pope every Thursday;

and the Cardinal secretary of the Holy Office has an audience on the second Sunday of every month.

THE CONSISTORIAL CONGREGATION

If the Holy Office assists the Pope in the exercise of his supreme *magisterium,* or teaching authority, the Sacred Consistorial Congregation, which can be called the Church's ministry of the episcopate, assists him in the exercise of his supreme responsibility for pastoral care. The name refers to past practice, when all the preparations for decisions then taken in the plenary assembly of the Cardinals, the consistory, were made in this congregation. It was inevitable that the congregation should lose its original importance as the consistory came to be deprived of its earlier power. In the great curial reform of St. Pius X, however, new responsibilities of great importance were assigned to it under its old name; and the relationship with the consistory is still preserved since it is there that the appointment of bishops is formally confirmed. Its responsibilities now consist primarily in making sure that the obligations binding diocesan Ordinaries are fulfilled; in recommending the appointment of bishops or the confirmation of their election; and in creating new dioceses and ecclesiastical provinces and dividing those already in existence. The episcopal power, which inside the diocese is independent – that is, not derived from the pontifical power – and which thus forms an essential element in the structure of the Church as founded upon divine law, finds its limits in this congregation, in subordination to the Holy See. The formal material for the supervisory authority which is thus exercised by the Consistorial Congregation lies in the reports, answering detailed questions, which all the bishops of the Latin Church throughout the world have to submit in rotation – those of Italy in the first year, of Belgium, France, Britain, Holland, Ireland, Spain and Portugal in the second year, of the remaining European countries in the third year, of the Americas, North, South and Central, in the fourth year, and of Africa, Asia and Australia in the fifth year. In these quinquennial reports the bishops have to render a full and careful account of the condition of their dioceses – religious, administrative, financial and disciplinary – and of their relations with the civil authorities. These reports are carefully studied, and may lead to further enquiries; criticism may be made, or certain measures may be prescribed, or perhaps a visitation may be ordered. The European bishops are obliged to come personally to Rome, *ad limina apostolorum,* "to the threshold of the apostles", in the year in which they make their reports; and bishops residing outside Europe have similarly to visit Rome in alternate report-years – that is, every ten years.

The competence of the Consistorial Congregation extends only to the territories of the Latin or Western Church in which the hierarchy is fully established. In other words, it does not extend to the Eastern Churches in communion with Rome, or to any of the territories which are under the jurisdiction of the Church's "ministry of the missions", the Congregation for the Propagation of the Faith. So far as the appointment of bishops is concerned, the Consistorial Congregation deals only with those cases where no diplomatic agreement with the civil authorities is involved. Where diplomatic intervention is necessary appointments are dealt with by the Congregation for Extraordinary Ecclesiastical Affairs; and in these cases the question is a somewhat complicated one, since the legal conditions for the appointment or selection of bishops vary from country to country. In principle it is the right of the Pope to appoint the bishops, but that right is restricted by agreements which have been made with various countries, as well as by the partial right of election enjoyed by some cathedral chapters and by the right of civil governments to raise political objections.

The Pope himself is Prefect of the Consistorial Congregation, as he is of the Holy Office, and is assisted by a

Cardinal as secretary. This in itself indicates the important position in the Curia which this congregation occupies. In order to ensure harmony in the decisions taken, so vital amid the great complexity of the affairs of the Church, the Cardinal Secretary of the Holy Office, the Cardinal Secretary of State and the Prefect of the Congregation of Seminaries and Universities are *ex officio* members of the Consistorial Congregation, and their representatives are attached to it as consultors. The assessor of the Consistorial Congregation is by tradition also the secretary of the College of Cardinals. The plenary meeting of the congregation takes place at the Vatican every Thursday.

The Congregation of Sacramental Discipline

One of the busiest congregations is that of Sacramental Discipline, which was first instituted by St. Pius X in the curial reform of 1908. Its competence extends to all territories of the Latin Church for decisions and legislation in all matters concerning the rites and ceremonies to be observed in the preparation, administration and reception of the sacraments. (The dogmatic aspect of the sacraments is the concern of the Holy Office, the liturgical aspect that of the Congregation of Rites.) One of the most important and most frequent duties of the Congregation of Sacramental Discipline is to take decisions when application is made for dispensations from impediments to marriage or when there is doubt about the validity or nullity of a marriage. It also handles cases concerning the validity of ordination to the priesthood and the sacrifice of the Mass. It can accordingly be called (in a certain sense and if what is sought is an aid to the memory rather than a comprehensive definition), the Curia's "ministry of law". It reaches its decisions through its own administrative machinery, referring the more difficult cases to the tribunal of the Roman Rota.

THE CONGREGATION OF THE COUNCIL

If the Consistorial Congregation may be called the Curia's "ministry of bishops", then the Congregation of the Council is that ministry which is concerned with the clergy and faithful of the Western world. To give only a few examples of its duties, it issues instructions for the observance of the rules of fasting and abstinence, for the observance of Sunday as a day of rest, for the sanctification of Sunday, for the dress of the clergy, for Mass stipends and for pious endowments. It exercises authority also over pious associations and over the administration of ecclesiastical property. Its original task, as its name indicates, was to carry out the reforms of the Council

71

of Trent so far as they affected the clergy, the people and
the Roman Curia, and that purpose survives to this day
in its duty of examining the acts of councils, provincial
synods and episcopal conferences. The Congregation of
the Council has a wide field and a correspondingly large
number of officials, and it was further enlarged by Pius XI,
who added to it a department for the furtherance and
supervision of popular religious instruction.

THE CONGREGATION FOR THE AFFAIRS OF RELIGIOUS

This congregation may be called the ministry of religious
orders. Within the Latin Church, and with the exception
of religious who work as missionaries and come under
the Congregation for the Propagation of the Faith, the
Congregation for the Affairs of Religious is the competent
authority for all questions concerning the life of religious,
whether men or women, monks or friars, brothers or nuns,
and whether in solemn or in simple vows; their direction,
discipline and studies, their temporal goods, their rights and
their privileges. In addition it has competence also over
members of the secular third orders, or tertiaries. Just as
bishops have to report to the Consistorial Congregation,
so are the heads of religious orders obliged to submit
their quinquennial reports on the condition of the religious orders and congregations which they govern to the

Congregation for the Affairs of Religious. A special commission deals with applications for the foundation of new religious institutes and their statutes.

THE CONGREGATION OF RITES

"The sacred rites and ceremonies which the Church employs at the bidding of the Holy Spirit are for Christian people a valuable means of teaching; they are the confession of true faith and bear witness to the majesty of sacred things; they raise the minds of the faithful to the contemplation of the mysteries of religion and kindle in them the fire of devotion. We have appointed five Cardinals whose privileged duty it shall be to watch over the strict observance of the sacred rites." These are the words of the Bull of January 22, 1587, by which, Pope Sixtus V instituted the Congregation of Rites. The two duties which were then assigned to it have remained essentially the same to this day. It has to watch over the uniformity and safeguard the development of the rites and ceremonies of the Latin Church, and, secondly, it has the task of conducting processes for beatification or canonization. It also has authority in all matters pertaining to sacred relics.

The administrative body of the Congregation of Rites is divided into three departments, or sections. The first of these deals with causes for beatification and canonization. The most important figure in this section is the Promoter-General of the Faith, who in these processes argues the case against the Postulator, representing the interests of the Faith and the Church and acting as it were as *advocatus diaboli,* the devil's advocate, by bringing forward every objection that can be raised against a proposal for beatification or canonization. As in other congregations, a number of prelates are *ex officio* members of the Congregation of Rites, in addition to the consultors. These are the papal sacristan, a protonotary apostolic, the dean and two auditors of the Sacred Roman Rota, the Pope's theologian (who is also the Master of the Sacred Palace), the assessor of the Holy Office, and the head of the congregation's third section. In this third section, which was established by Pius XI in 1930, historical beatification and canonization processes are dealt with – that is those processes in which, as in the cases of Albert the Great, Joan of Arc and Thomas More, no living person could appear as a witness, and in which judicial proceedings have to be supplemented by the scientific researches of the historian. The revision of liturgical books, which often require critical examination of their text, is also assigned to this section. The second section, "For the sacred liturgy", deals, as the name of the congregation suggests, with the wide range of questions which have a bearing on the supervision of the rites and ceremonies of the Latin Church.

THE CONGREGATION OF THE CEREMONIAL

The Congregation of the Ceremonial has nothing to do with the administration of the Church as a whole. It is responsible for the ceremonies of the papal *Cappella* and the Vatican Palace, and resolves all questions of etiquette and precedence at the Pontifical Court.

THE CONGREGATION
FOR EXTRAORDINARY ECCLESIASTICAL AFFAIRS

This might be called the congregation for relations between Church and State; it will be discussed later on, when we are dealing with the papal Secretariat of State.

THE CONGREGATION OF SEMINARIES AND UNIVERSITIES

The Congregation of Seminaries and Universities, still sometimes referred to under its old name as the Congregation of Studies, can be regarded as the Church's "ministry of education". Save for the territories for which the Congregation of Propaganda and that for the Eastern Church are responsible, it has jurisdiction in all questions concerning the teaching, the professorial staff, the order of studies and the administration in all the educational institutes of the Church: the pontifical universities, institutes of higher learning conducted by the religious Orders, the national colleges in Rome, the Catholic universities and faculties outside Rome, and the seminaries in which priests are trained as well. Where Catholic faculties are attached to the state universities, the part played by the Church is governed by the Concordat between that country and the Holy See. The Congregation can confer honorary doctorates on eminent scholars; in England Dr. Frank Sheed is one of the very few laymen to be honoured with honorary doctorates in theology, but honorary doctorates in law are conferred on laymen more frequently. Before the reforms initiated by St. Pius X the seven protonotaries apostolic *de numero participantium* traditionally enjoyed the right to confer doctorates. The Cardinal Secretary of the Consistorial Congregation is *ex officio* a member of the Congregation of Seminaries and Universities, and his assessor is attached to it as a consultor, on account of the close connection between the work of these two congregations; conversely, and for the same reason, the Cardinal Prefect of the Congregation of Seminaries and Universities is always a member of the Consistorial Congregation and his secretary serves as one of its consultors. Similar personal links exist between other congregations whose fields of action are closely associated.

THE CONGREGATION FOR THE PROPAGATION OF THE FAITH

The Congregation for the Propagation of the Faith, known also from its Latin name as the Congregation of Propaganda, is placed between the Congregation of Religious and the Congregation of Rites in the Code of Canon Law when the terms of reference of these Roman Congregations are stated. It is discussed here in a different place because, like the Congregation for the Eastern Church which we will turn to next, it differs in character from the other congregations.

To call the Congregation of Propaganda the Church's "ministry of the missions" is to give only a very approximate idea of its responsibilities. It has within its competence not only the administration, expansion and protection of the whole missionary system of the Church but also the affairs of the Church in all those territories of the world in which the ecclesiastical hierarchy is either not yet erected or not regarded as sufficiently well established to be brought within the regular administrative order of the Church. Wherever an ecclesiastical organization is springing up for the first time, nascent or still youthful, and therefore requires special care, there the Congregation of Propaganda is the competent Roman authority, dealing with all questions which in the normal administrative order would be referred to other congregations. In cases where decisions on matters of faith or morals, on the application of the laws of marriage or on the liturgy have to be referred respectively to the Holy Office, the Congregation of Sacramental Discipline and the Congregation of Rites, the Congregation of Propaganda is the intermediary, passing them on. It is, therefore, not only the headquarters of the pioneer work of the Church but also the nursery in which tender young plants are cherished until they are able to flourish in the field.

All this applies not only to mission territories in the narrower sense but also to all those countries of Western civilization in which the ecclesiastical organization of a Catholic minority is not yet sufficiently developed for it to be brought within the general administrative structure of the Church. Until the curial reform of 1908, England, Scotland, Ireland, the United States, Canada and Newfoundland were all administratively under the Congregation of Propaganda; so was Luxembourg. Today almost the whole of Asia and Africa, Australia and Oceania, as well as parts of North and South America, are still under the Congregation of Propaganda. Because of the widely extended power which this Congregation wields in its special position, its Prefect has sometimes been called "the Red Pope", his robes being the scarlet of a Cardinal whereas the real Pope's robes are white. The close concern of the missionary system of the Church with the problems arising from the end of the colonial period and the penetration of communism in the formerly colonial territories means that the Prefect of the Congregation of Propaganda is also a figure of world-wide political importance.

Such a statement, however, must not be misunderstood. It was not by chance that the first foundations of the Congregation of Propaganda were laid in the age of the discovery and conquest of the new world. As early as 1568 Pius V set up a commission of Cardinals charged with propagating the Faith in the new overseas territories then being colonized by the Spaniards and the Portuguese. After various reforms, Gregory XV in 1622 turned this commission into a permanent congregation, at the same time redefining the principles and tasks of missionary propaganda. It was already clear that the Church was striving to keep the propagation of the gospel independent of the temporal urge for conquest. Against much resistance and many obstacles this policy was upheld; and in modern times Popes Benedict XV, Pius XI and Pius XII have given a new strength to it. The separation of the missionary system from the colonial imperialism of political powers of the old and new world and the planned recruitment and training of a native clergy and a native hierarchy in the missionary territories are the visible expression of this policy, which has been abundantly justified by the political independence movements of the coloured peoples, and which is now confronted by many new difficulties and problems in the encounter with communism in the missionary territories.

The Urban College of Propaganda, founded in Rome by Pope Urban VIII and named after him, is closely linked with the Congregation of Propaganda. One of the oldest pontifical institutes of higher studies, it is attended by young theologians from all parts of the world and, with its students of all races and colours, is an impressive illustration of the universality of the Church and at the same time one of the most important centres of missionary thought. In the past it was housed in the same building as the Congregation, in the Renaissance palace in the Piazza di Spagna. In 1931 it moved to new buildings on the Janiculum, for the financing of which there is good reason to be grateful to the late Cardinal Mundelein, Archbishop of Chicago, who was a former student of the college and who died in 1939. The palace in the Piazza di Spagna is still used for the administrative work of the Congregation of Propaganda. In the same building are also the offices of *Fides,* the international missionary news agency, and the headquarters of the two great missionary societies of the Church, the Pontifical Work for the Propagation of the Faith – familiarly known throughout the English-speaking world as the A.P.F. – and the Pontifical Work of St. Peter Apostle for the Native Clergy.

THE CONGREGATION FOR THE EASTERN CHURCH

The Congregation for the Eastern Church has a special position that is comparable in some ways to that of the Congregation of Propaganda. It is the central Roman authority for all those Eastern Churches which have ended their state of schism and returned to the unity of the Catholic Church while at the same time preserving their own rite, their own liturgical language and their own largely autonomous constitutions. Until 1917 all these Eastern Churches – which include only a small proportion of the Eastern Christians, most of whom remain in schism – were under the jurisdiction of the Congregation of Propaganda. Benedict XV detached them from it and set up a separate congregation in order to emphasize the dignity and importance of these ancient centres of Christian culture, and to increase their power of attraction in the eyes of those Churches of the East still living in schism. It was also intended thereby to give visible and external expression to the great aim of reunification with the Christian East, of healing the historic breach between the Churches of West and East.

For the same reason the Pope decided to serve himself as Prefect of the Congregation for the Eastern Church, whose jurisdiction covers all questions arising within the territories of the Eastern Churches, with the sole exception of questions of faith, which, as in the missionary territories, have to be referred to the Holy Office. Since many of the Eastern Christians in communion with Rome now live under Communist rule, notably in the Western Ukraine, the Congregation for the Eastern Church, like the Congregation of Propaganda, is brought up against the great international issues of our time. The adherents of the dissident Churches of the East – and the word "dissident" is preferred to the harsher term "schismatic" – are estimated to number about a hundred and fifty millions, but those of the Eastern Churches in communion with Rome are fewer then ten millions. Among the latter five major groups are to be distinguished:

1. The Alexandrian rite, with fewer than 100,000

adherents, in which are included the Coptic and Ethiopian branches.

2. The Antiochene or Syrian rite, with perhaps half a million adherents, including the Syrian, Maronite and Malankar branches.

3. The Armenian rite, with about 150,000 adherents.

4. The Chaldaean rite, with about three-quarters of a million adherents, with its Malabar branch in India.

5. The Byzantine or Greek rite, to which belong by far the greater part of all Eastern Christians in communion with Rome, numbering between seven and eight millions. To this belong Bulgarian, Greek, Hungarian, Italo-Albanian, Melkite, Rumanian, Russian, Ruthenian and Yugoslav branches. Among these the most numerous are those of the Ruthenian rite, mainly inhabitants of or exiles from the Western Ukraine.

The liturgical languages in use in these Churches include Coptic, Ethiopian, Syrian, Arabic, Armenian, Chaldaean, Old Greek, Old Slavonic, Rumanian and Hungarian.

The Oriental Institute in Rome, founded by Benedict XV, works in close collaboration with the Congregation for the Eastern Church and is a teaching and research institute for all religious questions concerning the Churches of the East. It also accepts, as students or research workers, members of the dissident Eastern Churches. The Pontifical Commission for Russia was created in 1925 as part of the Congregation for the Eastern Church and became autonomous in 1930, with the full powers of a separate congregation in matters affecting Russian Catholics. After the retirement four years later of its President, the French Jesuit Bishop d'Herbigny, with whose personality and methods it had been so closely identified, it was brought back again into the Congregation for the Eastern Church.

Briefly and broadly to sum up, therefore, we can classify the Roman congregations by saying that the Holy Office exists for the entire Church; the Congregation of Propaganda, save for the exceptions that we have mentioned, for missionary territories; the Congregation for the Eastern Church serves all the Churches of the East; and all the other congregations are concerned with the Latin Church alone.

5

THE TRIBUNALS

THE APOSTOLIC PENITENTIARY

IN addition to the congregations, tribunals and offices have similarly developed in the Roman Curia in the course of history. The highest of the tribunals is the Apostolic Penitentiary, which, as the supreme "court of mercy", is a tribunal of a special kind. No names are entered in its acts or proceedings, and it issues no documents on which any external legal claim could be based. In this tribunal the Church exercises her jurisdiction "of the internal forum", *in foro interno,* granting absolutions and dispensations and deciding cases of conscience. A confessor who is in doubt and needs advice, or a confessor who in a case of particularly grave sin or one where ecclesiastical punishment arises cannot give absolution or dispensation himself, because only the Pope can do so, places the case, without disclosing the name of the penitent concerned, before the Apostolic Penitentiary, and obtains a decision or authority from it. The Apostolic Penitentiary can grant dispensations from "occult" or secret impediments to marriage; can validate marriages retrospectively, if they have been invalid because of an "occult" impediment; can for sufficient reasons dispense from vows and from obligations arising from oaths, or convert them into other obligations; and, in general, can give decisions on all questions of conscience. A special section deals with the granting and application of indulgences, the dogmatic aspect of indulgences being reserved to the Holy Office. The proceedings of the Apostolic Penitentiary are free of all charges, and, as with the seal of confession, are conducted with strict guarantees against any violation of secrecy.

Presiding over the Apostolic Penitentiary is the Cardinal Grand Penitentiary, *Penitenziere Maggiore*. On Maundy Thursday and Good Friday he may be seen seated in St. Peter's, wearing his ermine-trimmed cappa magna and with the *ferula* or wand in his hand lightly tapping the heads of the faithful thronging the basilica as they kneel in turn before him in order to gain indulgences. The same ceremony may be witnessed on Palm Sunday in St. John Lateran and on the following Wednesday in St. Mary Major. The assistants of the Grand Penitentiary still retain their traditional titles: the Regent, who supervises the administrative work of this tribunal; the Theologian, whose office is traditionally held by a member of the Society of Jesus; the Datary, the Corrector, the Sealer *(Sigillatore)* and the Canonist.

The position of the Grand Penitentiary is not relinquished with the death of the Pope. Written communication between the Cardinal Grand Penitentiary and the members of his staff is even allowed to continue during the conclave; nor does this correspondence, which bears the official seal of the Grand Penitentiary, have to pass through the censorship which examines all other correspondence leaving or entering the conclave. Should the Cardinal Grand Penitentiary die during the *sede vacante* period the College of Cardinals has the power immediately to elect a successor. All this is expressly laid down so that matters of conscience shall suffer no delay.

THE ROTA AND THE SEGNATURA

The two real tribunals of the Curia are the Rota and the Segnatura. The Sacred Roman Rota is a college of prelates consisting of fifteen judges or auditors with a dean at their head. Judgments are given by three auditors or, in particularly important cases, by all of them together, *videntibus omnibus*. It is a court of appeal from the diocesan courts. In certain cases it is also a court of the first instance; and in addition it is a court of appeal in civil and criminal cases from the court of the first instance of the Vatican

City. The origin of the name of the Rota is disputed. One theory, advanced by the German Cardinal Franz Ehrle, is that it is derived from a rotating desk at which documents used formerly to be brought before the auditors; another theory is that it comes from the circular chamber in which the auditors used to meet.

The most important decisions of the Rota are those taken in marriage cases. False notions about the practice followed in these cases are best corrected by the statistics which are published every year. Generally speaking, the marriage bond is upheld in rather more than half the cases heard and nullity is found in rather less than half. It usually happens that between a third and a half of the decisions are given without any fees being charged, when those concerned cannot afford to pay fees. From those who can afford them costs are required.

The Segnatura – or, to give it its full name, the Supreme Tribunal of the Apostolic Segnatura – is also a corporately organized tribunal, composed of a commission of Cardinals whose number is not limited – thirteen are listed in the *Annuario Pontificio* of 1959 – and who form the ultimate court of appeal in the Latin Church. It can hear appeals from judgments of the Rota, and its decisions are final. Its preparatory work is done by two colleges of prelates, the *prelati votanti* and the *prelati referendari.*

"Segnatura" is an Italian word; the Latin word *signatura* first occurs in the twelfth century as a term referring collectively to the curial officials whose duty it was to inform the Pope on the subject of documents presented for his signature. When these prelates were later given judicial responsibilities the term continued to be used, and eventually it was applied to the supreme tribunal.

The consistorial advocates who appear in the public consistory and appear on certain solemn occasions in attendance upon the Pope are chosen from among the advocates entitled to plead before the Rota and the Segnatura. Three-year courses of study are conducted at the *Studio Rotale,* under the supervision of the Dean of the Rota and with one of the auditors as director, to train advocates for the Rota; the courses are also followed by other clerical students.

6

THE OFFICES

THE SECRETARIAT OF STATE

By far the most important and significant Office of the Roman Curia is the Secretariat of State, with the Cardinal Secretary of State at its head. It came into existence, historically speaking, as sovereign nation-states began to emerge and the unity of medieval Europe began to break up. Its establishment was largely responsible for the decline in the power of the consistory. The historical predecessors of the Cardinal Secretary of State were the secretary of the papal *camera secreta* and the Cardinal *nipote,* the "nephew" and special confidant of the earlier renaissance Popes, whose position gradually developed into an independent office of which the holder in modern times may be called the Pope's foreign minister, and also, in a certain sense, his prime minister.

As holder of this office the Cardinal Secretary of State is responsible for the papal diplomatic corps. He receives the diplomatists accredited to the Holy See and, verbally or by letter, instructs the envoys of the Holy See. Every morning he is received in audience by the Pope, and matters which have not already passed through his hands by virtue of his office, because of their political implications, concern him then as the Pope's principal adviser and right-hand man. This confidential position of the Cardinal Secretary of State is shown in various other ways too. He lives in the Vatican, in close proximity to the Pope; he is a member of all important congregations; he vacates his office on the death of the Pope, so that the new Pope shall be free to choose the man to whom he feels best able to give his confidence.

The organization of the Secretariat of State is closely associated with the Congregation for Extraordinary Ecclesiastical Affairs. The Cardinal Secretary of State is prefect of this congregation, and he alone decides what work it shall undertake. Its administrative system, which is headed by a secretary, is at the same time the first section of the Secretariat of State, the section for extraordinary affairs. "Extraordinary" in this context refers, it should be explained, to the affairs of the Church in her relations with civil governments, by contrast with her own internal affairs, which are known as "ordinary". This section of the Secretariat of State for Extraordinary Affairs is concerned with the appointment of bishops in those countries where such appointments are regulated by a concordat, or with the erection or delimitation of dioceses where for one reason or another the agreement of the civil government is required, or with any matter of importance, such as the negotiation of a concordat, in which the assistance of the Congregation for Extraordinary Affairs is needed. The field of action of the different sections of the Secretariat of State is not rigidly defined, however, and it is left to the Cardinal Secretary of State and his closer assistants to decide upon the departmental organization. These closer assistants include also the head of the second section, known as the Section for Ordinary Affairs, who holds the title of *sostituto,* or deputy of the Secretary of State, for Ordinary Affairs. The third section is known as the Chancery of Briefs, and at its head is the Chancellor of Briefs; this has nothing to do with political matters, but is an authority concerned with the despatch of papal briefs in which also the final decisions of other departments of the curia are brought together, so making it easier to oversee and control the administration of the curia as a whole. In addition this third section is responsible for the conferring of papal orders and honours.

So wide is the experience gained by a Cardinal Secretary of State in his close relationship with the Pope that it might well be thought that he would be the Cardinal most likely to be chosen to succeed the Pope. In fact, however, the opposite is the case; only very rarely in history has it happened that a Cardinal Secretary of State, vacating his office on the death of the Pope, has himself been elected Pope, and when in 1929 Eugenio Pacelli, then Nuncio in Berlin, was brought back to Rome and made a Cardinal, becoming a few weeks later the Secretary of State of Pius XI, it would have been very reasonable to conclude that he had no chance whatever of becoming a future Pope. Tradition at least pointed the other way; not since 1667, when Clement IX succeeded Alexander VII, had a Cardinal Secretary of State become the successor of the Pope under whom he had served. In the conclave of 1939, however, the Cardinal Secretary of State, Cardinal Pacelli, was elected at the third ballot, when, receiving the necessary two-thirds majority, he took the name of Pius XII. Even in the Church, it is clear that the power of tradition is not insurmountable; as indeed Pius XII confirmed by dispensing altogether with a Cardinal Secretary of State during the last fourteen years of his pontificate. After his election he appointed the former Nuncio to Paris, Cardinal Maglione; but Cardinal Maglione died in 1944, and thereafter Pius XII left the heads of the first two of the three sections of the Secretariat of State jointly in charge. These were Monsignor Dome-

93

nico Tardini and Monsignor Giovanni-Battista Montini, responsible respectively for Extraordinary and Ordinary Affairs. Both were offered and declined the purple in 1953, as Pius XII afterwards revealed; they were both given the title of Pro-Secretary of State, with precedence between a Cardinal and a Patriarch. In November 1954 Pius XII made Monsignor Montini Archbishop of Milan; and both he and Monsignor Tardini became Cardinals in the consistory which followed soon after the election of John XXIII four years later. John XXIII lost no time in making Cardinal Tardini his Secretary of State and so reviving the full significance of an office which Pius XII had found unnecessary.

Embassies or legations at the Holy See are maintained by most European States on this side of the iron curtain, and by nearly all the Latin American countries, as well as by the United Arab Republic of Egypt and Syria, Iran, Lebanon, India, Pakistan, Indonesia and Japan, by the Formosan Chinese, and, among the Africans, by Ethiopia and Liberia. It was in the later middle ages that the Holy See for its part began to send permanent diplomatic representatives to civil governments. These are known as Nuncios, and the Secretariat of State is responsible for them. It is their duty under the present Code of Canon Law to maintain and cultivate good relations between the

Holy See and the civil governments to which they are accredited, and in addition to watch over the life of the Church in the countries in which they serve and to give regular accounts of their stewardship. They are, therefore, not only diplomatic representatives, to whom relations between Church and State are entrusted, but also ecclesiastical representatives of the central Roman authority. They have the diplomatic status of ambassadors and, under the provisions of international law, enjoy the privileges and immunity enjoyed by diplomatic representatives.

A Nuncio is doyen of the diplomatic corps in the capital in which he serves, but an Internuncio does not have that privilege. Whereas a Nuncio corresponds to an ambassador, an Internuncio corresponds to a minister plenipotentiary, heading a mission which corresponds not to an embassy but to a legation. Although these envoys must watch over the welfare of the Church in the countries in which they serve, the authority of each bishop is supreme within his diocese and the envoy of the Holy See cannot encroach upon his jurisdiction. In the order of precedence Nuncios and Internuncios, who are always archbishops, rank above local archbishops and bishops but not above Cardinals. Apostolic Delegates also are permanent papal envoys, but their duties are purely ecclesiastical, with clearly defined powers and no diplomatic status. They are in general appointed only to countries which do not maintain permanent diplomatic relations with the Holy See, like the United States, Canada, Mexico, Australia and Turkey. Britain, on the other hand, has a permanent Legation at the Holy See but receives only an Apostolic Delegate in London; and Switzerland receives a Nuncio at Berne but maintains no mission at the Holy See at all. Apostolic Delegates are by no means always under the Secretariat of State; depending on the territory to which they are assigned, they can be under the Consistorial Congregation, the Congregation of Propaganda or the Congregation for the Eastern Church. Yet the position of an Apostolic Delegate can sometimes be more important politically than that of a Nuncio, as is indicated by the fact that the Apostolic Delegate to the United States is usually made a Cardinal at the end of his term of office, whereas that distinction is by no means always conferred upon Nuncios. No Cardinal ever serves as the permanent envoy of the Holy See, but papal Legates, *Legati a latere,* are Cardinals who are given special powers and sent as the personal representatives of the Pope on certain missions. The Pope is usually represented by a Legate at Eucharistic Congresses or major ecclesiastical celebrations. Sometimes a curial Cardinal is sent from Rome as a Legate, and sometimes a

Cardinal residing locally is appointed. The honorary title of *Legatus natus* is attached to certain sees, including Cologne, Salzburg, Esztergom (the primatial see of Hungary), and Gniezno (the ancient primatial see of Poland), but these carry no powers with them.

The *Accademia dei Nobili Ecclesiastici* was founded in Rome in 1701 to train those intended for the diplomatic service of the Holy See, which was confined in those days to the sons of noble families. Many great diplomatists have been produced by this Academy, including in more recent times such Popes as Leo XIII and Benedict XV and such Secretaries of State as Cardinal Rampolla, under Leo XIII, and Cardinal Merry del Val, under St. Pius X; while Pius XII taught there as professor of ecclesiastical diplomacy from 1909 to 1914. The privileged position of the noble families has now disappeared, however, and only a small proportion of those attending the *Accademia dei Nobili Ecclesiastici* nowadays are in fact *nobili*. Moreover, outstanding figures from other departments of the service of the Church are more and more often chosen for important positions in the diplomatic service; so it was when the future Pius XI, a scholar who had become Prefect of the Vatican Library, was chosen at the end of the first world war to be Nuncio to the newly-restored Poland, a diplomatic mission of the first importance at that time.

The Vatican's daily newspaper, *L'Osservatore Romano,* and the weekly *Osservatore della Domenica,* come under the general supervision of the Secretariat of State. *L'Osservatore Romano* was founded in 1861 by Marcantonio Pacelli, the grandfather of Pius XII, and is printed at the Vatican. The relationship of these newspapers to the Secretariat of State should be determined very cautiously. Within the limits prescribed for it *L'Osservatore Romano* is independent and unofficial save for the formal announcements which it carries in the column headed "Nostre Informazioni". The Vatican makes use of the paper to record official news – the list of those received each day by the Pope, occasional statements from the congregations, tribunals and offices of the Curia, announcements of the appointments of bishops and so on – without being responsible for the editing of the news columns. The only official journal of the Roman Curia is the *Acta Apostolicae Sedis.*

The Vatican's broadcasting station, to which powerful new transmitters were added a year before the death of Pius XII, is directed by the Jesuit Fathers and counted among the technical services of the Vatican City State. It is of course at the disposal of the Secretariat of State and other central authorities and institutions of the Church for their special requirements as these arise.

THE APOSTOLIC CHANCERY

The Roman Curia includes other departments in addition to the Secretariat of State which are technically classed as Offices, but in these other Offices it is usually only a name which survives to recall a significance held in the past but now lost. The Apostolic Chancery, for instance, was originally the effective central authority of the Curia, and its head, the Chancellor of the Holy Roman Church, held a position which could be compared in many ways to that of a papal prime minister. Its main function today is the drafting and despatch of papal decrees and bulls concerning appointments made in the Consistorial Congregation, the establishment of new dioceses or cathedral chapters, and other matters of ecclesiastical importance. The head of the Chancery is always a Cardinal – the Cardinal Chancellor who serves as notary to the consistory. In addition to the officials of the Chancery, he is assisted by the college of the Protonotaries Apostolic *de numero participantium.*

THE APOSTOLIC DATARY

The Apostolic Datary also, under the Cardinal Datary, used to have in the past a very considerable power which it no longer retains. Its origins go back to the time when papal documents already signed only became effective when they were dated. The duty of dating them lay with an official known as the *Datarius,* whose office also dealt with petitions and the granting of favours. Nowadays his duty is to examine the qualifications of those who apply for non-consistorial benefices – that is to say, those benefices in which the right of appointment is reserved to the Pope personally.

The Apostolic Camera

In the earlier centuries it fell to the Apostolic Camera – originally the "chamber" in which ecclesiastical vestments, altar-plate and relics were kept – to administer the property and revenues of the Holy See. Its head, the Cardinal Camerlengo, could accordingly be described as the papal minister of finance. The name remains as an honorary title, but in normal times the Cardinal Camerlengo no longer has anything to do with financial administration. He is in charge of the temporal goods and rights of the Holy See only during the *sede vacante* period, between the death of one Pope and the election of the next. During the Pope's lifetime only the high rank of the dignitaries of the Apostolic Camera recalls its once powerful position. The Vice-Camerlengo, the Treasurer-General and the Auditor-General have the same rank as the Major-Domo of His Holiness: they belong to the so-called *fiochetti* or tassel prelates who in bygone days shared the privilege of the Pontifical Court of decorating the harness of their horses with violet-coloured silk tassels. How important the holders of these offices were is made clear by the fact that they were all included in the ministry of the States of the Church which Pius IX set up under the terms of the constitution of 1847. The Camerlengo then became Minister for Commerce, Agriculture, Art and Science; the Vice-Camerlengo was Governor of Rome and Minister of Defence; the Treasurer-General was Minister of Finance; the Auditor-General was Minister of Justice. These past glories of the Apostolic Camera are also reflected in the honorary rank of its college of *prelati chierici*.

The Finances of the Holy See

The property and revenues of the Holy See are now no longer administered by the Apostolic Camera but by two separate bodies, which, however, work in close association with one another and with the Vatican bank. None of these publishes any accounts. The *Amministrazione dei Beni della Santa Sede* is responsible for current domestic expenditure and is under a small commission of three Cardinals assisted by a number of laymen, experts in finan-

101

cial matters. The revenues which it administers include income from the property and capital investments of the Holy See, the fees charged for various services performed by the Roman curia, the fees charged when orders and decorations are conferred, occasional gifts or legacies, and, finally, the so-called Peter's Pence, the income provided by the voluntary contributions and collections of the Catholic faithful all over the world; those well placed to know say that this last source of income varies greatly from year to year. No taxes are levied by the Holy See.

The *Amministrazione Speziale della Santa Sede* has a different function. It also is under a small commission of Cardinals – often the same ones – and is similarly assisted by a professional staff of lay specialists whose experience in financial matters is equalled only by their discretion. It is responsible for the funds which the Italian Government paid to the Holy See as compensation for the loss of the city of Rome, under the financial agreement which was part of the Lateran Settlement in 1929. The assets of this *Amministrazione* were originally worth 1,750 million lire, of which 1,000 million lire were in Italian State bonds and 750 million were in cash. On the Italian side this was estimated at the time to be the equivalent of 450 million gold lire. What use may have been made of the cash, and what the total assets of this *Amministrazione* are today, is a matter for conjecture.

The Pope's private funds, mainly derived from personal gifts and legacies, are administered by the *Elemosiniere Segreto,* or Privy Almoner.

The Vatican City State has its own financial administration, deriving its revenues from administrative fees, from its postal and telegraph service – the sale of its own stamps being particularly profitable – from a surcharge on the retail prices of the monopoly which obtains all food and other goods tax and duty free, and from the money charged for admission to the Vatican Museum and Galleries. In addition it receives a subsidy from the *Amministrazione dei Beni della Santa Sede.*

THE SECRETARIATS OF BRIEFS

The other two Offices which remain to be mentioned have only minor importance. The Secretariat of Briefs to Princes – the reference is mainly to Princes of the Church – and the Secretariat of Latin Briefs draft letters and decrees on the instructions of the Pope and polish the Latin style of papal allocutions and encyclicals and similar documents. The Secretary of Briefs to Princes has for many years been Monsignor Antonio Bacci, an eminent Latinist who is not only the leading exponent of the older

103

tradition but is dedicated to the task of reviving Latin as a living language. To this end he has compiled an elaborate and ingenious dictionary to provide Latin words for all kinds of modern technical terms, and has also founded the quarterly *Latinitas* and built up an international circulation for it. The Secretary of Briefs to Princes and the Secretary of Latin Briefs are both privy chamberlains of the Pontifical Court. Just as numerous historical survivals in the names and duties of the curial Offices recall the past while no longer corresponding to the methods used in transacting the business of the Church, so also are many old traditions retained in these Offices, and successfully upheld in the conduct of day-to-day affairs against the pressure of the typewriter, the telephone and the telegraph. This is particularly true of the form in which written papal pronouncements are drawn up. We shall mention here only the more important of these.

There is a distinction in authority and in application to be made between Apostolic Constitutions and Papal Rescripts. An Apostolic Constitution has general application, whereas a Rescript is the reply of the Holy See to a question or request that has been submitted, and usually concerns only the person to whom it is addressed. The basic administrative laws of the Church are issued as Apostolic Constitutions: an example is the Apostolic

Constitution *Provida Mater Ecclesia* in which Pius XII in 1947 gave juridical status for the first time to what are known as Secular Institutes, whose members follow the religious life while still living in the world, without wearing a religious habit. When a papal decision concerns a matter of faith it is promulgated in a dogmatic constitution. A *Motu Proprio,* in which an administrative decision can also be expressed, is a decree which does not come, like a Rescript, in reply to a question or request, but is issued by the Pope on his own initiative, which is the meaning of the Latin words *Motu Proprio.*

When we come to papal letters there is a distinction to be made between Bulls, Briefs, and the various kinds of Apostolic Letters. The most solemn and weighty form of a papal letter is the Bull. This is drawn up in the Apostolic Chancery or the Datary according to the prescribed rules and is inscribed on a broad sheet of heavy parchment. Its name is derived from the leaden capsule – in Latin the *bulla* – in which the seal is enclosed. In very rare cases gold or silver is used instead of lead. The *bulla* is attached to the parchment by a silk or hempen cord – the silk cord for a "Bull of Grace" and the hempen for a "Bull of Justice". The leaden seal, however, is nowadays used only on very solemn occasions; red sealing-wax is generally used, or sometimes the seal is inscribed

105

with red ink. Like the leaden seal, it bears a cross, the heads of the apostles Peter and Paul, and the name of the Pope. A Bull is not signed by the Pope, but by the Cardinal Chancellor or Datary as the case may be.

A Brief is a less weighty and formal document, concerned with a less important matter. As its name implies, it is a brief document, shorter than a Bull, more concise, more sparing in its use of the elaborate language of the Curia. It usually announces the bestowal of some favour or some new appointment. It is written on fine parchment and is drawn up in the Chancery of Briefs, the third of the three sections of the Secretariat of State. A further characteristic of the papal Brief is the seal stamped upon it with the fisherman's ring that the Pope wears. The impression of the Pope's ring shows, with the name of the reigning Pope, a representation of St. Peter in his boat, casting his nets. The document bears the signature of the Cardinal Secretary of State or his representative, or of the Chancellor of Briefs.

All forms of papal letters which are not either Bulls or Briefs are included in the term Apostolic Letters. These are normally drawn up in the Secretariat of Briefs to Princes or the Secretariat of Latin Briefs. In their simplest form they can be congratulatory letters or messages, or acknowledgements of declarations of loyalty and devotion. If they bear the signature of the Pope, or are perhaps even written by him personally, they are known as autograph letters, or chirographs. An Encyclical is a special form of Apostolic Letter, discussing at length some topic of general importance and usually addressed to all the bishops, clergy and faithful of the world but sometimes to those of one nation or one region only.

THE COMMISSIONS OF CARDINALS

For special tasks, either permanent or only temporary in nature, new bodies have emerged in recent years from the organization of the Curia: commissions of Cardinals which are either dissolved when their work has been completed or continue on a permanent basis. Their duties and powers are separately defined in each case. Like the congregations, these commissions of Cardinals usually have a number of consultors and experts at their disposal. We have already spoken of the Pontifical Commission for Russia; other commissions of importance to the Church as a whole include the Pontifical Commission for Biblical Studies, the Pontifical Commission for the Authentic Interpretation of the Code of Canon Law, the Pontifical Commission for the Codification of the Canon Law of the Eastern Church, and, although this last differs from the others in character, the Abbey of St. Jerome for the Revision and Emendation of the Vulgate.

The Pontifical Commission for Biblical Studies – more tersely known as the Biblical Commission – was set up by Leo XIII in 1902, charged to promote the scientific study of Holy Scripture and to watch over the fruits of such study in the interest of the tradition of the Church and the purity of her teaching. In this sense and in its particular field it is an authority comparable to the Holy Office in being charged with vigilance for the faith. The Biblical Institute, which was founded by St. Pius X in 1909 as a centre for teaching and research, and which has a branch in Jerusalem, has, like the Oriental Institute, the status of a special faculty attached to the Pontifical Gregorian University, and is concerned with scholarship alone.

The Commission for the Authentic Interpretation of the Code of Canon Law was set up by Benedict XV in 1917 after the publication of the new Code of Canon Law for the Latin Church. Its duty is to ensure the uniform development and growth of the law of the Latin Church. It gives decisions on questions of interpretation and can in certain cases and with the permission of the Pope issue new decrees and have them incorporated in the Code of Canon Law.

The Commission for the Codification of the Canon

Law of the Eastern Church was set up by Pius XI in 1935; a great part of its work is now completed and published.

The Commission for the Revision of the Vulgate was originally a commission of Cardinals charged with a great work of scholarship, that of using the methods of modern textual criticism to restore the original text of the Latin translation of the Bible made by St. Jerome. That translation is known as the Vulgate because it has for many centuries been in common use in the Latin Church. But through all those many centuries its text has become changed and corrupted, so that its restoration was undertaken by a commission established by St. Pius X. Practical reasons led Pius XI to entrust this tremendous work, involving the comparison of many hundreds of texts, to the learned Benedictine monks of the abbey of San Girolamo, or St. Jerome, which he founded in Rome for this purpose and made immediately subject to the Holy See.

THE BUILDINGS OF THE CURIA

As the English translation of this little book is made, six congregations of the Roman Curia – those of the Consistory, the Sacramental Discipline, the Council, Religious, Rites, and the Seminaries and Universities – are preparing to move into the spacious modern quarters which have been prepared for them in the Palazzo Pio, facing the Piazza di San Pietro and within a few steps of the Vatican Palace itself. They are coming from the Piazza di San Callisto, on the right bank of the Tiber behind the picturesque Piazza di Santa Maria in Trastevere. The Congregation of Seminaries and Universities had been in the Palazzo di San Callisto for a long time when a new building was erected alongside it to house the other five of these congregations.

The principal building of the curial administration was earlier the Palazzo della Cancelleria, in the Corso Vittorio Emanuele, which used to accommodate most of the congregations but where only the administrative offices of the two tribunals of the Rota and the Segnatura now remain as guests of the Chancery. This magnificent Renaissance building, with a beautiful colonnade in its courtyard, was never very suitable for modern office-work; the Piazza di San Callisto was not very conveniently situated; and the new arrangements in the Palazzo Pio will be welcomed by all concerned, as well as making for greater speed and efficiency in the vast and ever-growing work which the congregations handle.

The Holy Office has a Palazzo of its own behind the colonnade of St. Peter's; and in what is now the Via della Conciliazione and used to be the teeming Borgo

110

stands the Palazzo dei Convertendi, once a hospice for converts and now the home of the Congregation for the Eastern Church and of the Apostolic Penitentiary. All the administrative work of the Church will be done, therefore, in close proximity to the Vatican Palace – the chief exception being that, as we have already noted, the Congregation of Propaganda remains in the Piazza di Spagna. The Datary is no longer of great importance but still has its old Palazzo on the slopes of the Quirinal Hill. The Cardinal Secretary of State, as we have seen, lives in the Vatican Palace, where the Secretariat of State and the Congregation for Extraordinary Ecclesiastical Affairs have offices on the third floor of the so-called Old Palace; they were temporarily installed there in 1870 when the Secretariat of State had hurriedly to leave the Palazzo della Consulta on the Quirinal Hill, and they have remained there ever since. Also in the Vatican Palace are the offices of the Apostolic Camera, the two Secretariats of Briefs and the Congregation of Ceremonial.

7

THE PONTIFICAL COURT

AFTER all that we have now said about the structure and work of the Roman Curia no doubt ought any longer to remain in any mind about the right view to take of the splendour and magnificence with which the Pope, as visible head of the Church and an independent temporal sovereign, is surrounded on great occasions. The pilgrim to Rome, however, who has perhaps on the previous day paid a visit to the catacombs and seen something of the hard, austere spirit of early Christian times, and then walks for the first time through the halls of the Vatican Palace on his way to an audience with the Pope, may feel at first disedified when he reflects on how far the history of the Church has travelled since the days of the catacombs. But he will soon realize that that progress has followed the same law of growth as the little seed which unfolds itself into the spreading branches of a great tree. The spectacle which the Vatican presents is not one of empty pomp; it all serves one great idea, and is the visible manifestation of a majesty which does not lose but on the contrary proclaims its meaning by being thus outwardly expressed.

Two bodies must be distinguished in the Pontifical Court: the *Cappella Pontificia* or Papal *Cappella,* and the *Famiglia Pontificia* or Papal Household. The Papal *Cappella* is composed of those dignitaries, ecclesiastical and lay, who take part in the sacred ceremonies in liturgical vestments or the uniforms proper to their office. It is the Papal *Cappella* which accompanies the Pope when he enters St. Peter's on such occasions as canonizations or when he takes part in some rite or function in the Sistine Chapel. Its functions are therefore liturgical. The *Famiglia,* on the other hand, is the Pope's household or court. The official list of those who are members of the *Famiglia,* however, may give an exaggerated idea of the papal court. In actual fact those who are regularly and daily in the immediate service of the Pope, performing duties in his household, are relatively few, and it is only on particularly solemn and splendid occasions that those other dignitaries and representatives who in the wider sense belong to the papal *Famiglia* perform any duties at the Pontifical Court. There are in addition offices of the papal household whose holders have nowadays hardly any duties to perform, so that they appear only on special occasions. There are others who have long since acquired full and exacting duties elsewhere and whose formal status in the court is no more than a mark of

113

special distinction. Of the domestic prelates and privy chamberlains of the Pontifical Court only very few perform any service there, the great majority being the bearers of purely honorary titles which in various grades and varieties derive originally from real offices at the court. This great majority are the Monsignori living and working all over the world. All through the lists of the members of the papal household one has to distinguish between those literally in the service of the household at the Vatican and those who hold titular positions conferred in recognition of their work and personal qualities.

THE PAPAL ANTICAMERA

The two members of the Pontifical Court who come first in rank are the two Palatine Cardinals, the Cardinal Datary and the Cardinal Secretary of State, whose functions in the curia have already been described. They hold only an honorary position in the papal *Famiglia,* the heart of which consists of the ecclesiastical and lay dignitaries of the *Nobile Anticamera Segreta:* the palatine prelates, the privy chamberlains participating, *Camerieri segreti partecipanti,* and the privy chamberlains *di spada e cappa,* of sword and cape. The principal palatine prelates in full-time attendance at the papal court are the Major-Domo and the *Maestro di Camera.* The Major-Domo,

114

who also holds the title of Master of the Apostolic Palaces, is the administrator of the papal household. The *Maestro di Camera* is in charge of all papal audiences; anyone wishing to be received by the Pope must apply to him, his name is printed on the cards giving admission to the great papal ceremonies in St. Peter's or the Sistine Chapel, and at the larger audiences it is he who presents the visitors one by one to the Pope. When the Pope is seated on his throne the *Maestro di Camera* stands to his left and the Major-Domo to his right. From 1929 until the election of John XXIII there was in practice no Major-Domo, and the offices of the two principal palatine prelates were combined in the person of the *Maestro di Camera* but John XXIII appointed a Major-Domo once again as soon as he had been elected, just as he appointed a Secretary of State once again. The *Maestro di Camera* became one of the so-called tassel prelates, the *prelati di fiocchetto* of whom we have already spoken, when he combined his duty with that of the absent Major-Domo. The other tassel prelates, as we have seen, are the members of the Apostolic Camera, and these do not belong to the papal *Famiglia* but to the *Cappella*.

The next two among the palatine prelates are the Auditor of His Holiness and the Master of the Sacred Palace; the latter is the Pope's theologian, and by long-standing tradition is always a member of the Dominican Order. Both of these now perform only limited duties in the papal court. The chief work of the Auditor is to serve as secretary to the Segnatura, the tribunal already described. The Master of the Sacred Palace was until 1925 the ecclesiastical censor for books printed within the diocese of Rome, and is an *ex officio* member of several of the congregations of the Curia.

Next in the *Anticamera Segreta* come the privy chamberlains participating, *Camerieri segreti partecipanti*. First among these is the Pope's private almoner, *Elemosiniere Segreto,* who looks after the Pope's private charitable work and is entitled to give the papal blessing in written form, as he does to great numbers of deserving people who frame it and hang it on their walls. He is followed in the order of precedence by the Secretary of Briefs to Princes, the Secretary of Ciphers – a senior official of the Secretariat of State, the Sub-Datary and the Secretary of Latin Briefs, all of whom are mainly concerned with administering the offices of which they bear the titles. The remaining privy chamberlains participating – the *Coppiere* or cupbearer, whose title has survived without his former duties; the Secretary of Embassies, whose duty it used to be to present himself to visiting sovereigns on their arrival in Rome; and the *Guardaroba* or keeper of the wardrobe –

116

do duty in the papal Anticamera in rotation, and have as private secretaries taken over some of the duties that used to be performed by the Pope's domestic chaplains, in looking after his private correspondence, writing letters and reporting on petitions of minor importance. Last in the order of the privy chamberlains participating comes the papal Sacristan, who serves also as the Vicar-General of the Vatican City and is traditionally a bishop and an Augustinian friar.

Whereas all the privy chamberlains mentioned so far have been prelates, the third group in the Anticamera consists entirely of laymen, the *Camerieri segreti di spada e cappa partecipanti* (privy chamberlains participating of sword and cape), who wear the traditional dress of the Spanish court, including the sword and cape by which they are known. At the head of this group, with precedence immediately after the palatine prelates, is the *Maestro del Sant'Ospizio,* a Roman prince whose duty it is to receive reigning sovereigns and heads of state at the foot of the stairs when they come to visit the Pope. Then comes the *Foriere Maggiore* of the Apostolic Palaces, which literally means quartermaster-general, representing the Major-Domo. He is followed by the *Cavallerizzo Maggiore,* or Prefect of the Stables, whose office has lost its meaning since the coming of motor-cars, since he is not responsible for the Vatican garages, and the *Sopraintendente Generale alle Poste,* or Postmaster General, whose office survives from the days of the States of the Church; both these are purely titular positions. The officers commanding the Noble Guard and the Swiss Guard are also included in this group. Mention should finally be made of two other honorary positions held by laymen, even though these are not members of the Pontifical Court. We refer, first, to the two Prince Assistants at the Throne, an hereditary position held by the heads of the two noble families of Orsini and Colonna, who occupy a place of honour in the papal *Cappella;* and, secondly, to the Marshal of the Conclave, an office traditionally reserved to the head of the Chigi family.

DOMESTIC PRELATES

The title of a Domestic Prelate is an honorary distinction conferred upon priests who, although only nominally associated with the service of the papal household, are thereby made members of the *Famiglia Pontificia.* Among those who receive this distinction are those archbishops and bishops, with the patriarchs at their head, who have been appointed by the Pope to be Assistants at the Throne; the Protonotaries Apostolic; the prelates belonging to the curial Colleges of the Prelature; Domestic Prelates who obtain the title by direct grant; and finally, those archbishops and bishops who were made Domestic Prelates before their episcopal consecration.

Among the Protonotaries Apostolic there are three groups. The first consists of the Protonotaries Apostolic Participating, of whom there are usually seven; they have many ecclesiastical privileges and rank between bishops and abbots in the order of precedence. They have occasionally to attest certain acts at the Apostolic Chancery, and they also serve as notaries in processes of beatification and canonization, but in most cases the greater part of their time is taken up with other work. The second group are the Protonotaries Apostolic Supernumerary, whose honorary title is never conferred alone but always in conjunction with some other dignity; the canons of the three patriarchal basilicas of Rome, those of St. John Lateran, St. Peter's and St. Mary Major – the fourth patriarchal basilica, St. Paul's-outside-the-Walls, being monastic – and the canons of certain cathedral chapters in Italy, come into this category *ex officio*. The third group, and very much the most numerous, those who compose it being scattered all round the world, is that of the Protonotaries Apostolic *ad instar*, whose position is an honorary one conferred on individuals by papal Brief and also conferred *ex officio* on the members of certain other cathedral chapters. There is a fourth group of titular Protonotaries,

119

to which all Vicars General and Vicars Capitular belong; but these are diocesan and not papal appointments, and members of this group do not belong to the pontifical household. These titular Protonotaries, who are not numerous, can also be created by Nuncios, and by the college of Protonotaries Apostolic Participating.

The curial Colleges of the Prelature, to which reference has been made, are three: the *Collegio dei prelati chierici* of the Apostolic Camera, and those of the *votanti* and *referendari* of the Segnatura; but the great majority of Domestic Prelates do not belong to any particular college; they are clergy in all parts of the world on whom the title has been conferred in recognition of particular merits.

All the ecclesiastical dignitaries of the papal household so far mentioned enjoy certain visible distinctions which vary according to their rank – notably a ceremonial dress in the violet colour that is used by bishops. The layman can easily distinguish them from bishops by remembering that only bishops wear the violet skull-cap and biretta. In other words, all the clerical members of the Pontifical Court whom we have so far mentioned are known collectively as the prelates *di mantelletta,* having the right to wear the violet mantelletta, an open sleeveless garment reaching nearly to the knees. The other clerical members of the Pontifical Court whom we have yet to mention

120

are known as the prelates *di mantellone,* and are distinguishable by their violet *mantellone,* a cloak reaching to the ankles, open in the front, and with no sleeves but a long band hanging on either side.

PRIVY CHAMBERLAINS AND PRIVY CHAPLAINS

As so often happens when a title becomes increasingly separated from an office, a number of titles in the Pontifical Court have developed with the passage of time out of the two senior classes of ecclesiastical and lay Privy Chamberlains Participating, whose bearers are in most cases only occasionally called upon to do service in the court, and are often not called upon at all. An exception is provided by the Privy Chamberlains who form the college of the Masters of Pontifical Ceremonies, and who regularly assist as such in the liturgical functions in which the Pope and the Cardinals take part. The prefect of this college has the right *ex officio* to the title of a Protonotary Supernumerary, and is therefore the only one in this category and in the categories which follow who is a prelate *di mantelletta.* Clerics on whom the honorary title of a Supernumerary Privy Chamberlain has been conferred have the right when present in Rome to take their occasional turns of duty in the papal Anticamera; so also have those bearing the title of Honorary Chamberlain *in abito paonazzo,* "violet-clad". Honorary Chamberlains *extra urbem* are altogether unconnected with the Pontifical Court, since the use of their title and the privileges which it carries are limited to the places outside Rome where they reside.

The lay papal chamberlains have similarly graduated ranks. There are both Privy and Honorary Chamberlains *di spada e cappa,* of sword and cape, the former usually selected from the nobility whereas the latter can be commoners. When on duty the Privy Chamberlains *di spada e cappa* wear a chain with a red medallion over their evening clothes or their Spanish court dress, whereas the Honorary Chamberlains *di spada e cappa* have a blue medallion. In each of these classes there is a small group of Privy Chamberlains *de numero,* about four or five, who perform regular duties, whereas the others, the Supernumerary Privy Chamberlains, are only called upon occasionally, when they happen to be in Rome.

The prelates *di mantellone,* the lower category, include also the four Privy Chaplains who in turn assist the Pope when he celebrates his daily Mass, and who recite the breviary and the rosary with him. In the past they also performed secretarial duties which now fall to the Privy Chamberlains Participating; instead of these they now have certain responsibilities in the administration of the

Vatican and the curia. Here also we find honorary titles whose bearers have no office: the Honorary Privy Chaplains, and the Honorary Privy Chaplains *extra urbem*. The two Privy Clerics, *Chierici Segreti di Sua Santità,* serve the altar in the Pope's private chapel, but their main duties lie elsewhere. The college of the papal Privy Chaplains, the dean of which is at the same time assistant keeper of the wardrobe, comes into prominence only on the occasion of major liturgical functions. The so-called Apostolic Preacher occupies an honorary office; he is always a Capuchin, and he preaches in the presence of the Pope and the assembled members of the Pontifical Court on the Fridays of Lent and the Sundays of Advent. The confessor of the Pontifical Court is traditionally a member of the Servite order.

These two members of religious orders conclude the list of ecclesiastical members of the Pontifical Court, but to complete the picture mention ought also to be made of the servants, among whom are the *Aiutante,* the *Sediari* who carry the *sedia gestatoria,* and the *bussolanti* or doorkeepers of the Vatican Palace.

THE PAPAL GUARDS

The most striking figures at the papal court are the members of the pontifical guards, whose staff and senior officers occupy a high position in the order of precedence. If the number of men serving in the pontifical guards is compared with the number of inhabitants of the Vatican City State it may be concluded that that State holds within its walls, relatively speaking, the strongest army in the world. And what a curious army it is! Most of its men go about their own affairs for the greater part of the year and only put on their uniforms in the Vatican when they begin their turns of duty. A soldier who has just been wearing a gleaming plumed helmet will go home wearing his soft felt hat. They are armed with halberds and swords, they wear steel breast-plates and have bayonets fixed to their unloaded rifles, but they have no machine-guns, no cannon – and certainly no tanks! Most of them receive no pay; and when their supreme commander passes they all go down on their knees. They have to do not only military exercises but spiritual exercises as well. St. Pius X once had a memorable conversation about this army with one of its commanding officers. During a time of crisis this officer had worked out a plan for the military defence of the Vatican and submitted it to the Pope. St. Pius X examined it and, pointing to one spot which was especially marked on the officer's map, asked, "And what does this mean?" The commanding officer replied that this was the proposed position of one of the guns; at which the Pope

asked, "But can one *shoot* with our guns?" The commanding officer was somewhat offended. "But of course,
Holy Father", he said. "If one can shoot with this gun",
the Pope declared, "it will have to remain in the cellar.
The Vatican shall not be defended with cannon". Critical
historians maintain that this conversation never in fact
took place; but, *si non è vero, è ben trovato*. Another story,
however, is well authenticated. In 1935 the world's press
reported that bomb-proof air-raid shelters were being
built in the Vatican as a precaution against possible air
raids. Pope Pius XI accordingly issued a statement which
was published in *L'Osservatore Romano,* saying that there
was no truth whatever in these reports; the Holy Father,
he added, was convinced that the dome of St. Peter's was
such a venerable monument of the Christian religion
that no civilized nation could conceivably make it a
target for attack from the air. And what is illustrated by
the story of St. Pius X and the cannon and by the affair of
the non-existent air-raid shelter also describes all the papal
guards: they have no military tasks. Their activities are
restricted to guard and police duties for the maintenance of
order and security within the Vatican City State.

First in dignity comes the Noble Guard, founded in
1801 as the Pope's *Guardia Nobili del Corpo,* or Noble
Bodyguard. Its members were chosen from the noble

families of the States of the Church, and they are still chosen from those families now, even though the States of the Church no longer exist. They provide the guard in the papal Anticamera, and escort the Pope when he leaves his private apartments to attend a public function. The full strength of the Noble Guard is about sixty, all of whom are officers; but it only appears in full strength on very solemn occasions. Its uniform is both magnificent and elegant, and is derived from that of the mounted body-guard of the kings of Spain. The Pope's Noble Guard was mounted up to the time of St. Pius X, and stabled its horses where the Vatican's printing-works now stands; its rattling spurs and high riding-boots still recall its former glory.

The quarters of the Noble Guard are on the same floor of the Vatican Palace as the papal reception halls, and contain a fine collection of weapons; these quarters resemble an aristocratic club more than a military barracks. Members of the Noble Guard composed both the papal march which is played during the solemn entrance of the Pope into St. Peter's and the *Largo religioso* which echoes from the dome of the vast basilica at the words of consecration in the papal Mass. The senior officers of the Noble Guard, ranking as generals and colonels, and the chaplain, have the rank of Participating Privy Chamberlains in the

126

order of precedence. Among them is also the *Vessillifero ereditario di Santa Romana Chiesa,* the hereditary standard-bearer of the Holy Roman Church, whose office is hereditary in the family of the Marchese Don Patrizio Patrizi. It is his privilege to carry the red star-spangled standard, which is so large that it cannot be completely unfurled unless the bearer is mounted on horseback. Its interest being historical rather than religious, it is kept in the Marchese's private palazzo in Rome.

The Standard of the Holy Roman Church, which was carried on the crusades in the Middle Ages, and which could be seen in the Corpus Christi procession in the Piazza di San Pietro up to the beginning of the last century, is to be distinguished from the yellow and white flag of the Pope and the Papal States, which was introduced by Pius VII as late as 1808. Pius VII did this in protest against an act of violence of the French, who had impressed the Roman militia into their own army. Before that time the papal colours were red and yellow, which are still today the colours of the City of Rome.

The Swiss Guard, recently increased in strength, now includes about a hundred and forty officers and men. It is so called because it has always been, and still remains, composed entirely of Swiss nationals, recruited since the beginning of the sixteenth century under agreements with the Catholic cantons of Switzerland which have been many times renewed. They live in barracks in the Vatican and usually enter the service on a two-year basis, although they can leave at two month's notice. It is the duty of the Swiss Guards to guard the gates of the Vatican City and the Apostolic Palaces, especially those giving access to or entry from the outside world; and they also do duty in the papal Anticamera. With their halberds, their slashed breeches and stockings of yellow, blue and red stripes, their white ruffs and steel helmets, with steel breastplates on state occasions, they are a picturesque survival of the times of the Medici Popes. The finest hour in the history of the Swiss Guards, the day never to be forgotten, was May 6, 1527, when they covered the flight of the Pope during the sack of Rome, and were massacred to a man in St. Peter's and in the piazza outside. To this day it is on May 6 that new recruits to the Swiss Guard are sworn in. The commanding officer of the Swiss Guard is a colonel who has the rank of a Privy Chamberlain Participating and is a member of the *Anticamera Segreta.* His deputy is really a lieutenant-colonel but is styled only lieutenant, *tenente,* just as the commander himself is styled only captain, *capitano comandante.* The spiritual care of the Swiss Guard is entrusted to a full-time chaplain who is also Swiss. The canteen of the

128

Swiss Guards used to be a great attraction to tourists, a romantic rendez-vous, up to the time of the Lateran agreements which constituted the Vatican City State in 1929, but since that time it has not been open to the public.

The Palatine Guard of Honour was established by Pius IX in 1850 and is a corps of volunteers about five hundred strong with a colonel as their commanding officer. They are recruited from the citizens of Rome and form a guard of honour at solemn papal functions; some of them also take turns of duty inside the Vatican Palace. They have their own part-time chaplain. Their great day comes on the Sunday after the feast of SS. Peter and Paul, when, dressed in the light blue breeches and dark blue tunics of their uniform, with their plumed bearskins, they march with sloped rifles behind their band, which leads them with joyful music into the Vatican gardens. There they assist at Mass before the replica of the grotto at Lourdes which was the gift of the French to Leo XIII, and, after an address from their chaplain and another from their commanding officer, new recruits are sworn in. Then follows the march-past of the entire corps, to the strains of the papal march. Then the rifles are stacked, the band begins to play less formal music, and the members of the Palatine Guard, together with their families and the people of the Borgo, enjoy a convivial garden party. They eat heartily, and many a glass of wine is drunk, and proud fathers of families have themselves photographed in their uniforms. "Splendid", said the popular Roman poet Giuseppe Belli (1791–1863) when he recognized a friend on one such occasion, "It was again splendid at your parade today. I once saw the changing of the guard outside the royal palace in London, but you are a lot better." And the guard so addressed, his heart swelling with pride as he sat eating his lunch, holding in his arms the youngest bambino who wanted to kiss his babbo in the fine uniform, replied, "You are right; we are more bloodthirsty."

The Papal Gendarmes were formed from the Pontifical Carabinieri raised in 1816 by Pius VII and subsequently disbanded. Most of them are professional policemen. In their full-dress uniform, with top-boots, white breeches and high bearskins, they resemble Napoleon's guards. They also are commanded by a colonel, and it is their duty to provide the usual police services in maintaining internal order and security in the Vatican City State. They are all carefully chosen men, and many of them have previously served with the Italian carabinieri. Their commanding officer is a former officer of the carabinieri. They have a part-time chaplain. There are also a small number of plain-clothes policemen and detectives in the Vatican City to assist the papal gendarmes.

The Noble Guard is under the patronage of St. Sebastian; the Swiss Guard is under the patronage of St. Martin, to whom their little church in the Vatican City is dedicated: the Palatine Guard have St. Peter as their patron, and the Papal Gendarmes have St. Michael.

PONTIFICAL ORDERS

As a temporal ruler the Pope has the right to confer membership in pontifical orders of knighthood and other honorary distinctions. The two most exalted pontifical orders enjoy an equal position in the order of precedence and have each only one class: these are the Supreme Order of Christ and the Order of the Golden Spur. Both are only rarely conferred, and are reserved almost exclusively for heads of states, heads of governments and members of ruling or formerly ruling houses. Much more frequently conferred are the Order of Pius, founded by Pius IX in 1847, the Order of St. Gregory the Great, founded by Gregory XVI in 1831, and the Order of St. Sylvester, also founded by Gregory XVI and called after Pope St. Sylvester I. Each of these has four classes: Knights Grand Cross, Knights Commander with and without Star, and Knights. The Knighthood Grand Cross in the Order of Pius is hereditary, but that is not the case with any other class in that order, or with any of the other pontifical orders of chivalry. The Order of St. Gregory the Great has a military and a civil division in each of its classes. Each order has its own uniform, which is worn on formal occasions. Among the less exalted papal decorations the most widely conferred are the cross *Pro Ecclesia et Pontifice* and the *Benemerenti* medal. The Golden Rose is in fact a spray of several roses, a delicate ornament in gold which can be conferred not only on individuals but also on churches and cities. It is generally reserved for sovereigns, and its costliness is not the least of the reasons why it is only rarely conferred.

When individual cases are regarded it will no doubt seem that the outward token of distinction by no means always corresponds to the personal merits of the recipient; but that is bound to be so, no less in the case of distinctions conferred by the Pope than with those conferred by temporal courts and heads of States. Not only personal merit but also the courtesies of political life and a respect for the written or unwritten social hierarchy determine the award of papal honours; it is bound to be so. For the lesser decorations the payment of fees alone often suffices, if a satisfactory recommendation can be produced. One

132

must not apply too strict a standard in a matter which is in the nature of things so closely bound up with human weakness and vanity. It has long been the general experience of the world that not every personal achievement is rewarded with honours and that not every honour is the reward for personal achievement; and so it is with papal honours also.

8

THE POPE'S DAILY LIFE

THE PRIVATE APARTMENTS

AMID the splendour of the Apostolic Palaces, the magnificence of the Pontifical Court, the Pope lives a lonely life; although John XXIII has contrived to make his somewhat less lonely than that of his predecessor. The authority and responsibility of his office preoccupy so completely the man who has become Pope that all private life comes to an end. In his relationship with those nearest to him a remoteness develops which even long-standing friendship can break down only in fleeting moments. Only in the German students' song does the Pope live "gloriously in the world". In reality the burden of his office weighs very heavily upon him. Among recent Popes there have been none who have not turned pale on having to don for the first time the white cassock which both distinguishes the Pope from all men and isolates him from all his brethren. From the Lateran agreements of 1929 until the election of John XXIII nearly thirty years later, the daily life of Pius XI and Pius XII retained with little relaxation the pattern which the life of Pius IX had assumed when he was made a "prisoner in the Vatican" in 1870. Earlier in his pontificate Pius IX had known the days when the Pope resided alternatively either in the Vatican or in the Quirinal Palace; when he drove in a state coach through the streets of Rome; when he visited the major basilicas on the great feast-days of the Church; when he gave his blessing from the portico of St. John Lateran or of St. Mary Major; when he opened new buildings in the city or unveiled new monuments; or when he visited the homes of the noble families of Rome as a guest. All of this was wholly out of the question for Leo XIII and his successors; until John XXIII, within a few weeks of his election, began to show in striking fashion and to the great pleasure of the Roman people that he was not going to regard himself as a prisoner of the Vatican in any sense. Leo XIII spent almost his entire life as Pope in two rooms on the second floor of the Vatican Palace overlooking the Cortile di San Damaso. Anyone received in private audience in his study at noon could see in the anteroom a little table with his simple midday meal upon it, covered with a napkin. This was the room in which the Pope also slept. St. Pius X especially suffered through his captivity in the Vatican, being filled with nostalgia for the open spaces of the Venetian Plain. He

135

found it hard to bear the restrictions imposed by the conventions of the papal court, and used to call the officials of the court his gaolers. He permitted himself a little modest latitude by having the third floor converted into private living-quarters for himself; it was there that the Cardinal Secretary of State had previously lived, and there that Cardinal Sarto, the return half of his ticket from Venice still in his pocket, lived during the conclave which elected him Pope. Downstairs the guards and chamberlains followed him like shadows as soon as he left the private library where he received those who called upon him, but up here at least he could have his meals in peace and spend some time in the evening with his Venetian chaplains. If convention prescribed that the walls of the audience halls on the second floor had to be lined with red damask, up here at least he could furnish his rooms in accordance with his own unpretentious taste. His successors gratefully took over these arrangements, and the modern pilgrim in the Piazza di San Pietro gazing at the lofty palace behind the colonnade can easily identify the windows that he sees; the row on the third floor are those of the Pope's private apartments, and those on the second floor are the windows of the audience rooms. Since the accession of St. Pius X the Cardinal Secretary of State has occupied the first floor.

The imprisonment of the Popes in the Vatican is over now, but the life led in these rooms has not changed much. Political chains have been lifted, but the Pope is still bound by the traditional chains of convention. And even if he tried to rid himself of these there would still remain the binding rules to which he must subject himself if he is to find time to keep abreast day after day with the exacting duties of his office. For the Pope could not get through his day's work without strict and detailed planning. It is recorded that Pius XI, when on one occasion he wanted to give particular care to the personal composition of an important document, found that he could only make time for it in his crowded day's programme by rising at four o'clock in the morning every day for a week.

THE BEGINNING OF THE DAY

The Pope habitually leaves his bedroom on the third floor before seven o'clock in the morning. His day's work begins with prayer and meditation and the celebration in the private chapel on the same floor of a Mass which is served by the Privy Chaplains in turn. Immediately after his own Mass the Pope assists at the Mass of thanksgiving celebrated by one of the Privy Chaplains. The breakfast which then follows, and which in accordance

137

with Italian custom consists only of milky coffee with some bread, does not take up much time. At half-past eight the Pope enters the lift which takes him down to the private library on the second floor in which he both works and receives those who come for private audiences. This is a large room with three windows looking down on the Piazza di San Pietro. Before the middle window is a large desk with a crucifix upon it, and also a telephone and a lectern. There are various pictures on the walls. There are many bookshelves, and all the books in these are bound in white; the books used to change with every Pope who worked here, but Pius XI, who, as an ex-librarian was familiar with the handling of books, had a systematically classified working library arranged, which included all the reference books most likely to be needed, and this has been retained ever since. The lift which brought the Pope down from the third floor had been used a few minutes earlier to bring the Cardinal Secretary of State up from the first floor, for it is he who has the first and most important audience of the day, which is usually also the longest. He informs the Pope about the state of current business, the course of any negotiations that may be in progress, the reports that have come in from Nuncios and other envoys of the Holy See. He makes proposals for appointments in the service of the Holy See, he tells the Pope

138

about the latest diplomatic developments, he produces drafts for treaties, notes and instructions. He draws the Pope's attention to important events in any country which may have a direct or indirect bearing on the interests of the Church; in short, he brings under review all the many problems that have been exercising his own attention in the Secretariat of State. The whole world comes before the eyes of these two men in this audience, as they discuss and consider each problem until at length the Pope reaches his decision.

THE ANTE–ROOMS

The Cardinal Secretary of State is less restricted by the rules of etiquette in his relations with the Pope than anyone else. He has special access, and can call on the Pope and discuss matters with him at any time of the day when important events demand it. All other visitors have to follow the ceremonial procedure of the papal court and to make their appointments in advance through the *Maestro di Camera,* who decides the date and time of the audience according to a fixed plan and with the agreement of the Pope. Nobody can be admitted without a card from the *Maestro di Camera,* whose offices are on a mezzanine floor adjoining the landing on the stairway which, immediately behind the celebrated bronze doors, leads down to the Cortile di San Damaso. The arrival, by motor-car or

139

on foot, of the visitors whose names appear in the list of the day's audiences, can be watched from the early morning onwards in the Cortile di San Damaso. They include Cardinals in their purple, bishops and prelates in their violet cloaks, priests in the usual street dress of the Roman clergy, with the round flat hat and the wide black cloak, members of religious orders, laymen in full evening dress whatever the time of day, ladies dressed in black and wearing veils, diplomatists in their court uniforms, nuns and, towards noon, groups of pilgrims from all parts of the world. From the Cortile di San Damaso they ascend the stairs, pass the Swiss Guards on duty outside the reception rooms of the Cardinal Secretary of State, and eventually, on the second floor, cross the threshold of a large hall where more Swiss Guards are on duty. This is the Sala Clementina, a spacious hall in the Renaissance manner with a gleaming marble floor, fine mosaics in colour, magnificently decorated vaulting and large mural paintings showing scenes from the life and legends of the martyred Pope Clement I. In the wall which faces the entrance is a fireplace, and to the left of that is a door which leads into the Consistorial Hall.

Servants clad in red damask escort the visitors to the cloakrooms, through a door to the left of the entrance, which leads to the loggias. Opposite this, to the right of

140

the Sala Clementina, is the door which gives access to the papal ante-rooms. The Swiss Guard standing beside it presents arms the minute he hears the rustling silk of a prelate's cappa magna. When a Cardinal approaches all the Swiss Guards on duty in the Sala Clementina present arms in salute. Most visitors have to wait in the Sala Clementina or in adjoining rooms until their turn comes. Before they reach the Pope's study they pass through ten more rooms, some large and some small. First comes one in which are the servants; then comes the Swiss Room, where Swiss Guards are on duty at night and two gendarmes during the day; then comes an L-shaped room with a detachment of the Palatine Guard; then the Gobelin room containing the duty officers of the Swiss and Palatine Guards. After this is a room in which officers of the Noble Guard are on duty, and in which one may see a large mural painting of the International Eucharistic Congress held in Vienna in 1912: the Blessed Sacrament is carried by the Dutch curial Cardinal van Rossum, and behind him the Emperor Francis Joseph is seen riding in a coach and wearing the white uniform of a general. In the adjoining throne room the senior officers of the Swiss Guard and the Honorary Chamberlains may be seen. It is in this throne room that the Pope receives diplomatists who come to present their credentials, and that he hears the Advent and Lenten sermons of the Apostolic Preacher.

Through another door, guarded by two Noble Guards with drawn swords, one enters the private ante-chamber, where one will usually find the officer of the Noble Guard who is on duty that week, with two Privy Chamberlains *di spada e cappa* who are likewise doing their turn of duty that week and who accompany the visitors from there onwards. For very grand audiences, such as the visit of a reigning sovereign, the traditional officers of the Pontifical Court are assembled in this room – the *Maestro del Sant'Ospizio,* the *Foriere Maggiore,* the *Cavallerizzo Maggiore* or Prefect of the Stables, the *Sopraintendente Generale alle Poste* or Postmaster-General, and the *Capitano Comandante* of the Swiss Guard, all of whom have been briefly described earlier in these pages. Only three more rooms now remain before the doors of the Pope's study are reached: the Hall of the Popes, the Hall of St. John, and the small throne room. In the second of these rooms, where Leo XIII used to take his meals and where he also slept, the Privy Chamberlain Participating on duty is seated at a small desk and it is he who presents the visitor to the Pope – unless the *Maestro di Camera* escorts him in person into the presence of the Pope. The last room, the small throne room, is that in which the Pope holds those

142

audiences to which he wishes to give a solemn but at the same time informal character. And here at last is the door of the Pope's study.

Private Audiences and Audiences "di Tabella"

When the Cardinal Secretary of State has finished his daily report to the Pope a bell is rung in the anterooms. This is the signal for the beginning of the audiences *di tabella,* which Pius XII discontinued in his later years but John XXIII resumed. These are the private audiences in which the Cardinals and prelates of the curia, the Prefects, Secretaries and Assessors of the Roman Congregations, the heads of the Offices, Tribunals and Commissions, come to report to the Pope on their work and to obtain the decision of the supreme ruler of the Church in all questions of importance. Such audiences follow a *tabella* or time-table worked out for a year in advance by the *Maestro di Camera.* Once again the sorrows, problems, cares and disappointments of all the world are brought before the eyes of the Pope.

But this does not conclude the list of private audiences. Others who follow are the Cardinal Vicar of Rome, to whom the Pope has delegated the administration of the diocese in which he is the bishop; the Privy Almoner, of whom we have already spoken, who submits petitions;

143

the Governor of the Vatican City State; the directors of
the Vatican Museums, the broadcasting station, and
L'Osservatore Romano; the Prefect of the Vatican Library;
the rectors of the pontifical universities, and of the national
colleges in Rome; superiors-general of the religious
orders; and, last but not least, the diplomatic envoys
accredited to the Holy See, who are received fairly regularly. In addition visitors arrive daily from all corners of
the world: bishops who have come to pay their quinquennial visits *ad limina,* vicars and prefects apostolic from
the missionary countries, nuncios and apostolic delegates,
statesmen, artists and scientists who happen to be in
Rome, princes and potentates, kings and presidents and
maharajahs and all those whose position demands the
courtesy of a visit or who have something of importance
to bring forward. Not all those whom we have mentioned
come on the same day, of course, but there are every day
at least six names on the list of private audiences, and with
every name the Pope must focus his attention on some
new personality and background, some new situation.

The Public Audiences

By the time the private audiences are over the cannon
fired from the adjacent Janiculum hill which announces
noon to the Romans has boomed over the city. Then the

public audiences begin, and these often occupy several hours. Hitherto the Pope has been wearing simply his white cassock with its short shoulder-cape, a sash of white silk with gold fringes at its ends and, probably, red shoes with a gold cross embroidered upon them. Now he takes a sleeveless red coat and a flat red hat with an upturned brim adorned with a golden cord; or it may be that these are carried for him by a servant in evening clothes. On particularly solemn occasions the Pope may wear the red ermine-trimmed mozzetta, a cape reaching to the elbows with a hood at the back. The so-called *camauro,* a little square red velvet cap which can cover the ears, not infrequently seen in old pictures of Popes – in, for example, Velasquez' famous portrait of Innocent X – has been revived by John XXIII, having before his time been seldom worn by modern Popes. As soon as the Pope leaves his study the clerics and laymen of the Pontifical Court who are on duty take their place in the retinue: the *Maestro di Camera,* the clerical and lay Privy Chamberlains, the officers and men of the pontifical guards. Meanwhile all those who are to be admitted to the semi-private and public audiences have been formed in groups and are waiting in the anterooms and the rooms adjoining.

The semi-private audiences are not very different from the private ones; the Pope stays a little longer than at

the public audiences; everyone there is personally presented to him, and with some of them he converses briefly.
Newly-married couples have a place of honour at these
audiences; they are among the Pope's visitors almost
every day, having been given this special privilege by
Pius XI in 1932. They do not require the special recommendation that others seeking audience must have; it is
enough for them to present proof of marriage at the office
of the *Maestro die Camera*. There are days when up to two
hundred newly married couples arrive at the Vatican not
only from Italy but from almost every country of the
world. The Pope usually addresses them, and gives a
medal to each bridegroom and a rosary to each bride.
When the Pope is at his summer villa at Castelgandolfo
these young couples are taken up into the Alban Hills in
buses at the Vatican's expense. Apart from the newly
married couples there are usually other groups also for the
Pope to welcome – nuns off to the foreign mission fields,
young theologians who are doing their studies at one or another of the national colleges in Rome, the participants in
some congress, the employees of some factory; the street-
cleaners of Rome or the tram-drivers of Milan; perhaps
a Canadian football team, or sailors from some ship that
is visiting the bay of Naples; the maid-servants of Rome,
who come on the feast of St. Zita, on April 27; farmers'

families from the Campagna bringing gifts of fruit from the country; parties of German pilgrims singing *Großer Gott, wir loben Dich* or of English pilgrims singing *God Bless our Pope;* pilgrims from America and Australia, France and Spain, India and China and everywhere else besides.

Every day the picture changes, and yet the procedure is the same with every group: the Pope walks along the rows of his visitors, who kneel before him and kiss his ring; an address of homage is either read or presented to him; and then the Pope, seated, speaks to them, thanking, encouraging and exhorting them and finally imparting the apostolic blessing. Very large pilgrimages, such as often bring thousands of pilgrims in a single party, assemble in special halls, and then the Pope is carried in on the *sedia gestatoria* so that all shall be able to see him. There is no very long tradition behind these daily public audiences at the Vatican, which were exceptional as late as the time of Leo XIII and were only made daily and, in fact, introduced in their present form by St. Pius X. Pius XI did all he could to encourage them; "These audiences", he once remarked, "are my window on the world."

THE POPE'S MIDDAY MEAL

The Pope takes his midday meal in his private apartments on the third floor of the Vatican Palace; but it is only very rarely that he is able to sit down to it punctually. The public audiences often last until two o'clock, and sometimes until three. Tradition ordains that the Pope shall take his meals alone, but St. Pius X disregarded that tradition, and John XXIII disregards it too. St. Pius X used to take his meals with the two Privy Chamberlains who had been his secretaries in Venice. His two sisters and his niece, who lived very simply in the nearby Piazza Rusticucci, used to attend his Mass on Wednesdays and Sundays and to take coffee with him afterwards; they were once invited to join him in a meal, but only once. Benedict XV sometimes had the company at table of his sister, the Contessa Persico. Pius XI got rid of the cook and the under-cook and put his former housekeeper from Milan in charge of the kitchen, and afterwards two Franciscan lay-brothers; but he revived the old tradition and never invited anyone to join him at the table, although the Privy Chamberlain on duty had to read the newspapers or his personal correspondence to him as he ate; the correspondence consisted mainly of petitions which he passed on to the office of the Privy Almoner. It is true that it did very occasionally happen that Pius XI invited a few people to breakfast, which hardly counted as a meal, usually on days when, as a special mark of distinction, he personally performed the episcopal consecration

148

of a prelate of the Pontifical Court or the Roman curia, or of a newly-appointed bishop from the mission-field; and then the Pope would sit apart from the company, on a little raised dais. Pius XII continued the practice of his predecessor in this matter, with very little change. The Vatican banquets to which the Cardinal Secretary of State invited diplomatic envoys in the name of the Pope became even less frequent than before, and in the time of Pius XII took place only once every few years. The Pope himself is never present at these banquets.

A Brief Respite

In the early afternoon one can hear a discreet clapping of hands in the Cortile di San Damaso. It comes from the papal gendarmes on duty, who thus announce that the Pope is preparing for his drive in the Vatican gardens. The signal is passed on, motor-cars are stopped and the gardens are closed to strangers. Presently the Pope appears, in white top-coat and red hat, and enters the waiting motor, together with the private secretary who is on duty. His drive is usually followed by a walk through the gardens. Leo XIII, whose landau used to be escorted by two mounted Noble Guards, was a great lover of the gardens. He took a personal interest in every detail of their arrangement, and since the summer villa at Castelgandolfo was deserted during the time of the "imprisonment in the Vatican" he had a little summerhouse built near the Leonine wall where he could spend his summer holiday. His successor, St. Pius X, was inclined to melancholy when he walked through the Vatican gardens; he disliked the symmetry with which the paths were laid out, he felt oppressed by the walls, he missed the open cross-country views to which he was accustomed from home, and when he heard the whistle of a railway-engine he would sadly say, "I wonder whether that is the train from Venice?" John XXIII does not conceal the same emotions. Benedict XV had grown used to the atmosphere of the Vatican City during his long years of service in the Secretariat of State and probably suffered least from the "imprisonment in the Vatican". He only went rarely into the gardens, usually to meet his brother, the Admiral della Chiesa. Pius XI, on the other hand, as an old mountaineer, was fond of longer walks, although as he grew older he used to remain in his motor-car. Pius XII availed himself only slightly and slowly of the new freedom of movement given to him by the Lateran agreements concluded by his predecessor; but John XXIII has availed himself of it as much as possible from the very moment of his election.

AT THE DESK AGAIN

After this break in the day's programme the Pope resumes his work. Private audiences begin again at about six o'clock, and public audiences also are frequently held in the evening. But even when there are no longer any visitors waiting in the anterooms a great deal still remains to be done. Documents requiring especially careful study and consideration may have been left on the desk in the morning; speeches and addresses have to be prepared, instructions to be given, important documents to be revised, letters to be written. These are the hours in which work is assigned to the secretaries. The American inventer – who was born at Milan, but Milan, Ohio – presented the Milanese Pope Pius XI with an apparatus that could record dictation, and this stood in the Pope's study for a long time. Occasionally the Pope would experiment with it, but in the end he gave it to the director of the Vatican broadcasting station, preferring to dictate in the old-fashioned manner, or to write with his own hand. The evening audiences and work at the desk occupy five hours, and it is not before half-past ten that the watcher in the Piazza di San Pietro can see the lights go out in the Pope's study. The Pope then goes again to his private chapel on the third floor for evening prayers; when these are over it is eleven o'clock. This period of

151

prayer is followed by another light meal, after which the Pope retires to his private rooms. But papers and books await him even there, and often several hours elapse before he can finally retire for the night.

DUM VOLVITUR ORBIS

One day is very much like another. Even the changes and variations in the daily progamme return with a certain regularity – when heads of state have to be greeted, or when ambassadors and other diplomatic envoys have to be received in solemn audience to present their credentials; when the Cardinals visit the Pope on Christmas Eve or the diplomatists come to offer their good wishes on New Year's Day; when on the feast of the Purification (February 2) the chapters of the major and minor basilicas of Rome, the Roman clergy, the Roman colleges and seminaries of all nations and all orders send their delegations to the Vatican to present the Holy Father with a heavy and richly-decorated candle; or when on the feast of St. Agnes (January 21) the Lateran choir brings to the audience-room from the church of Sant'Agnese *fuori le mura* two unspotted white lambs to be blessed by the Pope, before the pallia, the symbols of the archiepiscopal dignity, are woven from their wool; when the Apostolic Preacher delivers his Lenten and Advent

152

sermons; when a microphone is placed on the desk in the Pope's study so that he may deliver a broadcast address and impart his blessing, perhaps to a Eucharistic Congress in America or Australia; when a consistory has to be held or the meeting of a congregation has to be presided over; when a decree of the Congregation of Rites confirming the virtues of a servant of God has to be read in a process for beatification; when on the eve of the feast of SS. Peter and Paul (June 28) the Pope goes down into the *confessio* in St. Peter's to bless the pallia over St. Peter's tomb; or when a solemn Requiem Mass is offered in the Sistine Chapel on the anniversary of the death of the Pope's predecessor, or for the repose of the souls of the Cardinals who have died during the year, or when a Mass of thanksgiving is offered on the anniversary of the coronation of the reigning Pope, or on Maundy Thursday and Good Friday or for the solemn High Mass of Easter, or when a canonization is performed in St. Peter's – these are but examples of the constant round of great ceremonies which inevitably impose great physical strain upon the Pope.

Under the burden of the heavy pontifical vestments he could hardly take a single step without those who help to support their weight; for on these occasions the Pope wears, over his white cassock, an alb with cincture and

153

sub-cincture, a falda – a white silk vestment with a train, worn only by the Pope; a pectoral cross, a stole; then the tunic of a sub-deacon, the dalmatic of a deacon and the chasuble of a priest, with the fanon – another vestment worn only by the Pope – the pallium and the maniple; on his feet the high pontifical stockings made from a stiff material embroidered in gold; on his head the mitre or the triple crown known as the tiara – all this, as though to symbolize how heavily the burden of office can weigh upon a man.

The chief changes in the Pope's daily time-table occur on August 15, the feast of the Assumption, when the curial holidays begin. They continue until the end of October. The daily audiences *di tabella* cease, and the daily programme is a little less crowded. Since 1934, resuming the tradition of the years before 1870, the Pope has again gone up into the Alban Hills in the holiday period, to spend some weeks in the summer villa at Castelgandolfo. But there also, by the side of the volcanic lake where he has at his disposal instead of the Vatican gardens the magnificent parks of the Villas Barberini and Cibo, with a spreading view across the Campagna to the sea, the Sabine hills and the Eternal City – there also the daily routine is hardly less exacting than at the Vatican. Rome can be reached by motor-car in a bare half hour, the telephone and direct radio communication are also there, and there also, in consequence, the round of duties is unbroken. There it was that Pius XII died, early in the morning of October 9, 1958, anxious even on his death-bed to return to the work which never ceases for the Pope.

INDEX

156